HOW TO GET AHEAD IN BUSINESS

HOW TO GET AHEAD IN BUSINESS

Foreword by
Richard Branson

Edited by Professor Tom Cannon

Virgin

Dedicated to Harry Simons, who died suddenly aged 15 months in January 1993 from a rare metabolic disorder known under the collective name of Reyes Syndrome.

The Harry Simons Trust now exists to fund research into Reyes Syndrome.

Those wishing to know more about the Harry Simons Trust should contact:

> *Paul Simons*
> *Simons Palmer Denton Clemmow and Johnson Ltd*
> *19/20 Noel Street*
> *London W1V 3PD*

First published in Great Britain in 1993 by
Virgin Books
an imprint of Virgin Publishing Ltd
332 Ladbroke Grove
London W10 5AH

A catalogue record for this book is available from the British Library

ISBN 1 85227 423 9

Text design developed by Wilf Dickie and Roger Kohn

Typeset by Phoenix Photosetting, Chatham, Kent
Printed and bound in Great Britain by
Butler & Tanner Ltd, Frome, Somerset

Contents

Contents

Foreword
by Richard Branson

After leaving school aged sixteen to start *Student* magazine, I seem to have been much too busy with the practicalities of survival to read very much about the theory. As a result I have always believed that the only way of getting ahead in business is to get on with it and learn from one's own mistakes.

Having launched an advertising campaign to promote our airline under the title 'How to Get Ahead in Business', bookshops had thousands of requests for the book. So – being a businessman myself, and still determined to get ahead – I realized that there were plenty of people out there who felt they could learn something from others' experiences (and we – as the publisher – could get further ahead in business too!).

In fact we can all learn more by examining other people's failures, successes and general philosophy. I am the first to admit that it is much easier to follow a pioneer than to be a pioneer – in business or in everyday life – and that it should always be possible to avoid the pioneers' pitfalls by taking their advice. Even if the advice is as simple as 'If they get you down, sue the bastards!' as Sir Freddie Laker said to me ten years ago when we were starting Virgin Atlantic.

There is no doubt that the classic writings collected here for the first time by Tom Cannon contain perspectives and insights (most of which were new to me as well) from which every manager, entrepreneur or student can learn something.

It is also good to see the jokes in this collection. Because if Virgin has been about anything over the last twenty years, it has been about trying to be the best at what we do, but having fun at the same time!

How to Get Ahead in Business is an extraordinary collection of wit, wisdom and practicality to keep by the bedside, in the briefcase or just on the shelves as a ready reference to dip into.

If nothing else, have fun reading it!

Introduction

The introduction to this book is one of the most difficult things I've ever written. In part, this is because preparing the work has influenced and shaped my thinking about business and achievement far more than I ever expected. It was also because it is very daunting to try to draw together so many strands of insight, understanding and research in a few words. As I sat at my word-processor, unable to choose the right words, I decided it would be easier to write another book than give a brief introduction. Unfortunately, this comfortable belief is confounded throughout the book. Over and over again, complex and difficult ideas are summarized in a brief insight or penetrating observation.

I suppose this is one of the lessons we learn from looking at business success itself. Entrepreneurs, successful business people, innovators and leaders typically show a remarkable ability to take complex ideas and difficult concepts and create a novel, seemingly simple product, service or business. In preparing this book, I've concluded that good business writing brings out the elegant simplicity which underlies most business success. I've also learned from ploughing through vast quantities of business research, books and writing that it's much easier – or more common – to find writing that obscures rather than clarifies the routes to business success.

I find this both irritating and sad. Irritating because there is a great deal of excellent writing on business. Sad because business today offers so many exciting and fascinating opportunities. It is probably the last accessible opportunity for adventure which is available to most of us. Most of the geographical frontiers have been explored or require massive resources to reach. Science is increasingly a world of massive budgets and large teams. Sporting success almost inevitably goes to the specially endowed.

The business adventure is different. Almost every day, we hear of women and men who started this adventure with no obvious advantages but are now leaders in their community, industry or profession. Sometimes, they have a special insight into the needs of a particular group. Elsewhere, they recognize a trend. More often, they are determined to succeed regardless of the barriers they face and in spite of early or apparent failure. They might work for themselves or for others. This book is dedicated to these adventurers and those whose insights help us to understand their world. Their frontiers will never be conquered because their horizons are shaped by their spirit, imagination and skill.

Tom Cannon
Manchester, September 1993

★

Murphy's First Law
Nothing is as easy as it looks.

Murphy's Second Law
Everything takes longer than you think.

★

I would like to take this opportunity to thank the permissions departments of all those publishers who processed our requests to reproduce copyright material.

I'd also like to thank the many individuals throughout the Virgin Group and elsewhere who helped to bring this book into existence. I'll name a few specifically, starting with Gerard Kelly, who helped me with the research. I am also especially grateful to Paul Forty, Michelle Ogden and Rob Shreeve of Virgin Publishing for working round the clock (literally) to meet an apparently impossible deadline, as well as to Virgin's production manager, Gill Woolcott, and to Phoenix Photosetting and Butler & Tanner Ltd for all their efforts. And finally, my gratitude as always to my wife Fran for her constant patience and support. T.C.

1 My Way

Success Stories

It is not long since prevailing economic wisdom virtually discounted the entrepreneur as a key player in industrial or economic success. Global giants like IBM, General Motors, British Airways, ICI and BAT had such economies of scale and could deploy such vast resources that the entrepreneur was at best an historical curiosity. The Fords, Palmers, Singers might be interesting to the historian but no serious economist could pay them or their successor any attention.

This comfortable and convenient view of the world took into account virtually every aspect of economic theory. That is, apart from the annoying habit of entrepreneurs to challenge conventional wisdom and use their enterprise, determination and creativity to confound theory and change the rules. IBM now struggles to survive while Microsoft prospers. The famed committee systems of General Motors are battling to become more entrepreneurial. British Airways loses virtually every head-to-head against Virgin. ICI has been totally restructured to rekindle a spirit of enterprise. BAT was virtually moribund until Jimmy Goldsmith gave it a life-regenerating shock.

There are no simple and pat explanations to show how these and thousands of other entrepreneurs can rewrite the rules to succeed where others fail. Self-belief, determination and a refusal to be beaten, almost regardless of the odds, are part of the equation. Beyond these, the styles, approaches and backgrounds are almost as varied as the people themselves. As soon as a generalisation is produced, it is contradicted. They succeed, in part, because they are willing to take risks, but the survivors manage the downside to minimize their exposure. Many have little formal post-secondary education but they surround themselves with all the expertise they need. They might be ruthless in their determination to succeed but consistently highlight the importance of people to their success. Keeping close to their customers is a common theme, but most are willing to challenge the 'best' marketing knowledge – if their instincts tell them to. Their success probably lies in an ability to create a new reality from a mixture of the best of existing knowledge and their own insights.

★

To succeed you have to believe in something
with such a passion that it becomes a reality.
– Body and Soul *by Anita Roddick*

SELF-BELIEF

Self-belief is perhaps the single most important characteristic of successful entrepreneurs. Anita Roddick needed it to confound the accepted wisdom and scepticism of the cosmetics industry. Bill Gates shows it in his confident assertion that he will be a millionaire by the time he is 25 years old and his recognition not only that the personal computer miracle 'was going to happen' but that he was going to be part of that miracle.

Hard Drive: Bill Gates and the Making
of the Microsoft Empire
by James Wallace and Jim Erickson

Gates said he was heading off to Harvard in the fall. Then he added, in a very matter-of-fact way: 'I'm going to make my first million by the time I'm 25.' It was not said as a boast, or even a prediction. He talked about the future as if his success was predestined, a given, as certain as the mathematical proof that one plus one equals two. . . .

On a cold winter day in December 1974, Allen was walking across Harvard Square in Cambridge on his way to visit Gates, when he stopped at a kiosk and spotted the upcoming January issue of *Popular Electronics*, a magazine he had read regularly since childhood. This issue, however, sent his heart pounding.

On the cover was a picture of the Altair 8080, a rectangular metal machine with toggle switches and lights on the front. 'World's First Microcomputer Kit to Rival Commercial Models,' screamed the magazine cover headline.

'I bought a copy, read it, and raced back to Bill's dorm to talk to him,' said Allen, who was still working at Honeywell in nearby Boston. 'I told Bill, "Well here's our opportunity to do something with BASIC."'

He convinced his younger friend to stop playing poker long enough to finally do something with this new technology. Allen, a student of Shakespeare, was reminded of what the Bard himself wrote, in *Julius Caesar*; 'There is a tide in the affairs of men, which, taken at the flood, leads on to fortune. Omitted, all the voyage of their life is bound in shallows and in miseries. On such a full sea are we now afloat, and we must take the current when it serves, or lose our ventures.'

Gates knew Allen was right. It was time. The personal computer miracle was going to happen. . . .

Sometimes your friends and collaborators fall by the wayside. They lack the vision, the determination and the self-belief to sustain them. John Moores of Littlewoods showed this when, despite initial disappointment and strong advice to 'think things over' before going on, he committed all his savings to his new venture.

The Man Who Made Littlewoods
by Barbara Clegg

Back in Liverpool, John [Moores] and Colin [Askham] were joined by another friend from their Manchester messenger-boy days, Bill Hughes. The three young men were different in many ways; but what they had in common was a desire to make money. Discussing ideas and ways of achieving it was one of their favourite occupations after work had finished.

John had heard about something called a football pool being run by a man named John Jervis Barnard in Birmingham, but without any great success. Bill managed to get hold of one of Barnard's coupons, 'and late one night, when all the cable machines were quiet, we spread this thing out on his supervisor's desk and discussed it'.

Barnard had based his pool on the French *pari mutuel* system of betting, a long-established method in which ten per cent of the total stake is subtracted for management costs, and the rest goes to the winner, or is divided equally amongst the winners. John knew all about it, and for a while they amused themselves by working out just what Barnard would have to do before he started making a profit; how many coupons he would need and what the printing and distribution costs would be. It was not long before they decided that *they* could manage the whole thing much better.

Then suddenly they were in deadly earnest.

. . . Littlewoods Pools was started the next day. It was obviously going to be an expensive project and they decided that they would each have to put up £50 to start it off (£693 in today's values).

. . . They were all 'rather pale with excitement' as they met at the bank, each to draw out his £50. John described the feeling. 'As I signed my own cheque, my hads were damp. It seemed so much money to be risking.' . . . Just how risky it was, and how chancy the outcome, became apparent to the three young men very quickly. Of those 4000 coupons that John had urged his schoolboy team to hand out, only thirty-five came back. The bets totalled exactly £4 7s 6d (the equivalent of £74 now) and the first dividend was £2 12s (£44). The ten per cent deducted did not even cover their expenses; and they had to make good the deficit themselves, but they were determined to try again. Next time they had 10,000 coupons printed, which were all sent to a big match in Hull. Only one came back.

Before long they each had to put another £50 into the kitty. Halfway through the 1924–5 season they were still nowhere near paying their own way; indeed the top gross receipt for that first half, on 20 December, was £79 15s 6d (worth £1,358 today), out of which their ten per cent gave them the princely sum of just under £8. Then they each had to put in another £100 to pay Mr Bottomes' printing bill. It was all getting too much.

Just before Christmas, Bill called an emergency meeting of the triumvirate over canteen lunch and, keeping their voices down, they tried to decide what to do next. Bill, at least, had already decided.

'Let's face it,' he said, 'we've lost nearly £600 between us. It sounded like a good idea, but obviously it will never work. I vote we cut our losses and drop the whole thing.'

Colin nodded. It was sad, but he agreed with Bill. They both looked at John and waited for him to speak. He swallowed and took a deep breath.

'I'll pay you back what you've lost so far – that's £200 each – if you'll sell me your shares in it.'

They both looked totally shocked.

'I still believe in the idea,' he said stubbornly.

In no uncertain terms they told him how rash he was being, and asked him to think it over.

SCEPTICS

Confounding sceptics is of course par for the course with entrepreneurs. John Moores won backing from his wife when she said, 'I'd rather be the wife of a man who has gone broke than a man who is haunted by regret.' Alan Sugar's self-confidence, risk and backing took a different form. One suspects that his backer, Lalvani, was expecting to be confounded by the supremely confident and determined man who handed over the post-dated cheque.

Alan Sugar: The Amstrad Story
by Alan Sugar

Sugar was earning about £20 a week with Hensons, and he reckoned he could make that in a day on his own. He spent £80, the bare minimum, on a secondhand Mini-van and went to

Lalvani with a proposition. He was going to quit Hensons, so if he gave Lalvani a seven days' post-dated cheque for a couple of hundred pounds, would Lalvani give him goods to that value?

Lalvani hesitated. In those days John Henson was one of his best friends and the Binatone chairman was loath to be seen to be encouraging one of Hensons' workers to strike out in competition with him. 'Look, I'm going to quit, whether you help me or not,' Sugar said.

To satisfy his conscience, Lalvani suggested as a compromise that Sugar should go away for a couple of weeks' holiday before launching out on his own, so that it did not look as though Lalvani had directly encouraged him to make the break. Sugar agreed.

When the two weeks were up, Sugar duly presented Binatone with the post-dated cheque and collected his goods. Lalvani was surprised to see Sugar's van rolling into Binatone's premises that same evening: 'Give me the cheque back. Here's the cash,' Sugar said, handing over the money.

CAPABILITY

The kind of confidence shown by Alan Sugar produces results when it is underpinned by business skills and an ability to sustain and build a company. Alan Sugar's skills as a salesman meant he could clear his initial stock. The sustained growth of his firm relied on the ability to identify, develop and use a wide array of capabilities in himself and others.

The larger the firm and the more complex the products and technologies, the greater the demands for these abilities. They give master entrepreneurs the edge over their rivals. Perhaps the greatest business 'battlefield' of the first twenty years of this century occurred in the US car industry. Henry Ford won the first round because he could turn a vision into commercial reality. His early rival William Durant, the founder of General Motors, had the vision but could not match Ford's ability to mobilize resources and eventually to produce a car which was 'almost too good to be true'. In a host of ways (the push into international markets, branding, diversification), Durant's vision was nearer the truth. It is Ford, however, who is remembered, and William Durant died ruined by the Great Crash of 1929.

My Years with General Motors
by Alfred P. Sloan

No two men better understood the opportunity presented by the automobile in its early days than Mr Durant and Mr Ford. The automobile was then widely regarded, especially among bankers, as a sport; it was priced out of the mass market, it was mechanically unreliable, and good roads were scarce. Yet in 1908, when the industry produced only 65,000 'machines' in the United States, Mr Durant looked forward to a one-million-car year to come – for which he was regarded as a promoter of wildcat ideas – and Mr Ford had already found in the Model T the means to be the first to make that prediction come true. The industry produced more than a half-million cars in the United States in 1914. In 1916 Mr Ford alone produced more than a half-million Model T's and at his high point in the early 1920s he produced more than two million in one year. . . .

Both Mr Durant and Mr Ford had unusual vision, courage, daring, imagination, and foresight. Both gambled everything on the future of the automobile at a time when fewer were made in a year than are now made in a couple of days. Both created great and lasting lines of products whose names have been assimilated into the American language. Both created great and lasting institutions. They were of a generation of what I might call personal types of industrialists; that is, they injected their personalities, their 'genius,' so to speak, as a subjective factor into their operations without the discipline of management by method and objective facts.

★

Ford
by Robert Lacey

Now approaching his mid-forties — he celebrated his 45th birthday three months before the Model T was unveiled — Henry Ford was at the height of his powers. He had also consolidated control of his company and he had also consolidated control of himself. . . . He threw himself into every detail, insisting on getting small things absolutely right, going for innovation when it tested properly, but sticking to the tried-and-true when it did not. He never lost sight of the ultimate, overall objective. He had a vision of what his new car should look like. From all the improvisation, hard thought and hard work came a machine that was at once the simplest and the most sophisticated automobile built to date anywhere in the world. When advance circulars for the Model T were sent out to Ford dealers in the spring of 1908 the reception of the claims made on behalf of the car verged on incredulity.

'We must say it is almost too good to be true,' wrote a Detroit dealer to the company, while an Illinois agent seems to have treated the thing as a huge joke. 'We have carefully hidden the sheets away and locked the drawer, throwing the key down the cold-air shaft.' The dealer's anxiety appears to have been that if the Model T was really as good as Henry Ford said it was, and if his customers found out, then he would not be able to off-load his existing stocks of the Model N.

When the car finally went on the market at the beginning of October 1908, the wildest predictions were fulfilled. The first public advertisements for the Model T appeared on a Friday, and 'Saturday's mail,' reported the *Ford Times*, 'brought nearly one thousand enquiries. Monday's response swamped our mail clerks, and by Tuesday night, the office was well nigh inundated.'

Orders flooded in, with hard cash, and by the end of the winter Ford had to announce that the company could not take any more. They had sufficient advance orders to consume the entire factory output until the following August — and by the end of September 1909, more than 10,000 cars had been sold, bringing in over $9 million, a 60 per cent increase on the turnover of the previous year.

SERENDIPITY

Sometimes it needs outside support or intervention to break through the barriers to success. Henry Ford got it from a dentist called E. Pfenning who bought the first Model A car and stopped the haemorrhage of funds at the newly formed Ford Motor Company. Allen Lane's saviour came from an even more unlikely source. Lane was sure that his approach to paperback publishing was right. The rounds of conventional booksellers had ended in failure. It is impossible to predict the outcome if his bright idea of approaching Woolworths had produced the same response. Everything was pointing to failure as Prescott compared the dummy Penguin unfavourably with Woolworths own Readers Library. It is hard to imagine one of today's hard-nosed purchasing managers suspending judgement until their spouse had commented. Naturally, it helped that Lane and Prescott were old friends, but even today 'networking' is accepted as a key management discipline.

Allen Lane: King Penguin
by J. E. Morpurgo

That Allen Lane was the founder of the modern paperback is a claim made by many advocates over many years. . . . He developed the thesis that his series must be not only marvellously inexpensive but also, as a kind of compensation lest their economic presentation be regarded as expressing disdain, his books must be produced attractively, with dignity but in cheerful eye-catching format. He did not use the word 'packaging', which had not yet become a cliche, but the production doctrines which he was urging were significant far beyond the limits of book-publishing.

Disappointed by the reception he and Dick had faced from conventional booksellers but unwilling to accept the humiliation of failure, he had revived an idea that had fallen into desuetude in the months when he and Dick had been tramping round the bookshops. He would try to sell his books outside the customary boundaries of the book trade and, with that in mind, looked to Woolworth as a potential customer.

For many years books had been included in the variety of goods which Woolworth marketed at sixpence a time. Hitherto Woolworth had published on its own account a sixpenny reprint series. These books it had sold, exclusively in its own stores, to customers most of whom would never have risked exposing themselves to the patronizing airs of bookshop assistants.

Allen argued that his new Penguins were priced consistently with the Woolworth formula and presented in a manner that must make them suitable for display on the large open counters. They were patently goods that Woolworth could sell.

The firm's senior buyer did not agree. The dummy Penguin that Allen had thrust into his hand he compared unfavourably with books from Woolworth's own Readers Library; its paper cover and its severe design (the adjective amazed Allen) would not attract customers used to the brilliant pictorial wrappers and the elaborate if pseudo-William Morris embossed paper-board bindings of the Readers Library.

Prescott's rejection, so runs the story, was unhesitating, but because he was an old friend, he asked Allen to wait in his office to meet his wife who was expected at any moment. Mrs Prescott arrived, was shown the dummy Penguin, and unlike her husband, pronounced it delightful. Eagerly Allen offered her the list of prospective publications. She had not read one, she said, but she had no doubt that at sixpence a time she would risk buying the lot.

Grudgingly Prescott gave way to his wife's wisdom; he would take a few dozen of each title to try out in the principal Woolworth stores in London.

It was something, but it was not enough to save Penguin.

A few days later Prescott telephoned Allen. Would the Bodley Head accept a consignment order for Penguins? Allen agreed without hesitation and then rang up Sydney Goldsack, the sales manager at Collins, to ask him what Woolworth's meant by a consignment order. Goldsack explained that it involved sending stocks to every Woolworth store. 'What sort of numbers would this mean?' Allen asked. 'Hard to say,' replied Goldsack, 'but certainly not less than fifty thousand and could be a hundred thousand.'

Less than a fortnight after the meeting in Prescott's office, the Woolworth consignment order was confirmed at 63,500 copies. Mrs Prescott's intervention had been responsible for a sale that virtually matched all other pre-publication sales achieved hitherto in Britain and abroad. This one order brought Penguin within sight of the break-even point.

Lane's 'good luck' was the product of hard work and determination. He accepted Samuel Smiles' injunction to self-help. He was not put off by early rebuffs. Most of all, he neither felt sorry for himself nor did he believe that success would come automatically or easily. Mr Biswas was willing to try but found persistence a different challenge.

The 'Make Your Own Breaks' Credo
Success is a matter of luck: just ask any failure.

★

Self-Help
by Samuel Smiles

Those who fail in life are, however, very apt to assume a tone of injured innocence, and conclude too hastily that everybody excepting themselves has had a hand in their personal misfortunes . . . some consider themselves born to ill luck, and make up their minds that the world invariably goes against them without any fault on their own part. We have heard of a person of this sort, who went so far as to declare his belief that if he had been a hatter people would have been born without heads! There is, however, a Russian proverb which says that Misfortune is next door to Stupidity.

★

A House for Mr Biswas
by V. S. Naipaul

He stayed in the back trace and read Samuel Smiles. He had bought one of his books in the belief that it was a novel, and had become an addict. Samuel Smiles was as romantic and satisfying as any novelist, and Mr Biswas saw himself in many Samuel Smiles heroes: he was young, he was poor, and he fancied he was struggling. But there always came a point when resemblance ceased. The heroes had rigid ambitions and lived in countries where ambitions could be pursued and had a meaning. He had no ambition, and in this hot land, apart from opening a shop or buying a motorbus, what could he do? What could he invent? Dutifully, however, he tried. He bought elementary manuals of science and read them; nothing happened; he only became addicted to elementary manuals of science. He bought the seven expensive volumes of *Hawkins' Electrical Guide*, made rudimentary compasses, buzzers and doorbells, and learned to wind an armature. Beyond that he could not go. Experiments became more complex, and he didn't know where in Trinidad he could find the equipment mentioned so casually by Hawkins. His interest in electrical matters died, and he contented himself with reading about the Samuel Smiles heroes in their magic land.

WHAT IT TAKES

The entrepreneur's checklist opposite is designed to help the reader understand their own capabilities and the extent to which they have the range of attitudes and skills needed to start on the demanding road to entrepreneurial success.

Enterprise
by Tom Cannon

An entrepreneur's checklist

'Can we predict whether someone *has what it takes*?' A score of less than 100 suggests that major personal development is needed to cope with the demands of individual enterprise.

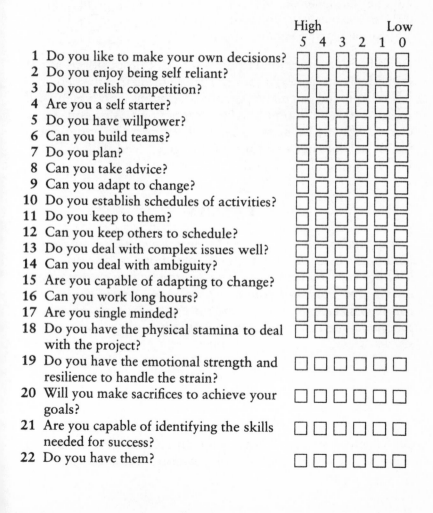

		High					Low
		5	4	3	2	1	0
1	Do you like to make your own decisions?	☐	☐	☐	☐	☐	☐
2	Do you enjoy being self reliant?	☐	☐	☐	☐	☐	☐
3	Do you relish competition?	☐	☐	☐	☐	☐	☐
4	Are you a self starter?	☐	☐	☐	☐	☐	☐
5	Do you have willpower?	☐	☐	☐	☐	☐	☐
6	Can you build teams?	☐	☐	☐	☐	☐	☐
7	Do you plan?	☐	☐	☐	☐	☐	☐
8	Can you take advice?	☐	☐	☐	☐	☐	☐
9	Can you adapt to change?	☐	☐	☐	☐	☐	☐
10	Do you establish schedules of activities?	☐	☐	☐	☐	☐	☐
11	Do you keep to them?	☐	☐	☐	☐	☐	☐
12	Can you keep others to schedule?	☐	☐	☐	☐	☐	☐
13	Do you deal with complex issues well?	☐	☐	☐	☐	☐	☐
14	Can you deal with ambiguity?	☐	☐	☐	☐	☐	☐
15	Are you capable of adapting to change?	☐	☐	☐	☐	☐	☐
16	Can you work long hours?	☐	☐	☐	☐	☐	☐
17	Are you single minded?	☐	☐	☐	☐	☐	☐
18	Do you have the physical stamina to deal with the project?	☐	☐	☐	☐	☐	☐
19	Do you have the emotional strength and resilience to handle the strain?	☐	☐	☐	☐	☐	☐
20	Will you make sacrifices to achieve your goals?	☐	☐	☐	☐	☐	☐
21	Are you capable of identifying the skills needed for success?	☐	☐	☐	☐	☐	☐
22	Do you have them?	☐	☐	☐	☐	☐	☐

		High				Low
		5	4	3	2	1	0

23 Can you fill in any gaps in your skills
from elsewhere? □ □ □ □ □ □
24 Can you deal with the risk of failure? □ □ □ □ □ □
25 Are you skilled at networking? □ □ □ □ □ □
26 Can you keep your objectives in view □ □ □ □ □ □
despite distractions?
27 Do you know your goals? □ □ □ □ □ □
28 Can you communicate them to others? □ □ □ □ □ □
29 Can you handle several tasks at once? □ □ □ □ □ □
30 Do you separate *need to's* from *nice to's*? □ □ □ □ □ □

Underlying the questionnaire is a series of propositions about individual enterprise. At the core lies a notion that the person is self reliant, and can make personal decisions, enjoys being self reliant and is not intimidated by competition. Alongside these ought to be the capacity to be a self starter. The enterprising individual does not wait for others to give a lead. This reflects a well-formed and strong will.

DETAILS

The attitudes and skill needed by entrepreneurs are seldom as glamorous or exciting as those depicted in movies or popular writing. For Charles Forte, it meant standing on the pavement outside an empty shop counting passers-by. This willingness to roll their sleeves up, take on board the basics and understand the fundamentals is repeated in virtually every entrepreneur's success story.

Forte
by Charles Forte

Mornings, afternoons, and evenings, I would stand on the pavement outside the empty shop with a recording counter. I checked the number of people walking by. I counted the numbers in the queues at the nearby bus stop; I counted the students and teachers coming in and out of the polytechnic; and became increasingly convinced that this was the site for me.

Attention to the basics plus determination can produce a breakthrough even when rejection by 'professionals' undermines confidence. The story of 'Spindletop' is a tribute to stubborn determination and the ability to find just the right person to work with. It starts with Patillo Higgins, 'a one-armed mechanic and lumber merchant' who was convinced 'oil could be found'. He turned for assistance to Antony F. Lucas, a former officer in the navy of the Austro-Hungarian Empire. Lucas eventually found Guffey and Galey. Galey's instincts told him that Spindletop would be the 'biggest oil well this side of Baku', but the scale of their discovery far exceeded their wildest dreams.

The Prize
by Daniel Yergin

Lucas and Higgins made a deal, and the captain commenced drilling in 1899. His first efforts failed. More professional geologists ridiculed the concept. They told him that he was wasting his time and money. There was no chance that a salt dome could mean oil. Captain Lucas could not convince them otherwise. He was discouraged by the professionals' rejection of what he called his 'visions', and his confidence was shaken.

With nowhere else to go, Lucas went to Pittsburgh to see Guffey and Galey, the country's most successful firm of wildcatters. They were his last hope. In the 1890s, James Guffey and John Galey had developed that first major oil field in the midcontinent, in Kansas, which they sold to Standard Oil. Galey was the true wildcatter, the explorer. 'Petroleum had John Galey bewitched,' a business associate would later say. In turn, Galey had an amazing ability to find oil. Though he diligently studied and applied the geological theories of the day, some of his contemporaries thought he could literally smell oil. Quiet and low-key, he was unstoppable and indefatigable on the hunt. Indeed, the search for the treasure counted for him far more than the treasure itself. . . .

John Galey went to Beaumont and surveyed the area. As the drilling site, he chose a spot next to the little springs with bubbling gas that Patillo Higgins had found. He drove a stake into the ground to mark the spot. With Captain Lucas out of town at that moment hiring drillers, Galey turned to Mrs Lucas and said, 'Tell that Captain of yours to start that first well right here. And tell him that I know he is going to hit the biggest oil well this side of Baku.'. . . On January 10, the memorable happened: mud began to bubble with great force from the well. In a matter of seconds, six tons of drill pipe catapulted out of the ground and up through the derrick, knocking off the top, and breaking at the joints as the pipe shot further upward. Then the world was silent again. The drillers, who had scattered for their lives and were not sure what they had seen, or even if they had actually seen it, sneaked back to the derrick to find a terrible mess, with debris and mud, six inches deep, all over the derrick floor. As they started to clean the mess away, mud began to erupt again from the well, first with the sound of a cannon shot and then with a continuing and deafening roar. Gas started to flow out; and then oil, green and heavy, shot up with ever-increasing force, sending rocks hundreds of feet into the air. It pushed up in an ever-more-powerful stream, twice the height of the derrick itself, before cresting and falling back to the earth. . . .

Lucas 1 on Spindletop, as the well became known, was flowing not at fifty barrels per day, but at as much as seventy-five thousand barrels per day. The roar could be heard clearly in Beaumont; some people thought it was the end of the world. It was something never seen before anywhere – except in the 'oil fountains' of Baku. The phenomenon came to be called a gusher in the United States. The news flashed across the nation and was soon on its way around the globe. The Texas oil boom was on.

What followed was riotous. The mad scramble for leases began immediately, with some plots traded again and again for ever more astounding prices. . . . Soon, land that had only two years before sold for less than $10 an acre now went for as much as $900,000 an acre.

RISK

Wildcatters and financial speculators have a great deal in common. They take massive risks. They rely on a mixture of knowledge, instinct and the resolve to succeed. Each of these played a part in establishing the base on which Nomura Securities could grow to become one of the most powerful financial institutions in the world. Tokushichi Nomura II, the founder of Nomura, showed all these characteristics during the great 'bear' and 'bull' markets of 1906 and 1907 in Japan. He had prepared the ground long before this turn of events, by studying company affairs and trends far more closely than his rivals. He was, in effect, ready to 'ride his luck'.

The House of Nomura
by Albert Alletzhauser

In 1906 the Osaka stockmarket was in the midst of an unprecedented boom. . . . Nomura had no doubt that the 1906 bubble would burst. He and Hasimoto did some research and found close similarities with the conditions before the stockmarket plunge following the Sino Japanese War. They began to examine the daily data on the market closely as Nomura's scouts tracked the selling and buying patterns of major Osaka dealers. Then, on 10 December, they detected a subtle change, noting that a few big dealers had begun selling. That day Nomura took action and began selling out his long-term portfolio, eliminating one third of his holdings by the end of the week. At the same time, he started selling share futures short, betting that the market would fall and he would be able to buy back at a cheaper price. . . .

Although the market was still moving against him, Nomura stepped up the pace of his short selling. Inevitably, margin calls from the market traders who dealt for him began to arrive. Japanese investors at that time needed little cash to make vast speculations on the market. If they made money, everything was fine and the profits were added to their trading accounts. But if the market did not go their way, they needed to remit funds on a daily basis.

The money Nomura had placed on consignment was rapidly being whittled down, so that by early January the fretful brokers began to press him even more brusquely. Years later, Nomura recounted how he had hidden under his desk to avoid creditors. He eventually resorted to hiring a rickshaw for the day and furtively wheeling around the streets of Osaka – in the middle of winter – stopping in obscure back-street cafes where he was sure not to run into irate creditors or fair-weather friends from Kitahama. Tension mounted at Nomura Shoten as salesmen, clerks and secretaries realized their jobs were in danger unless the market began falling soon. But day after day it continued to rise.

Then, on a snowy 19 January, it happened: the market began to crack. Jitsusaburo [Nomura's brother] was first with the news. He ran in the snow from the stock exchange to Nomura's office, only to find Tokushichi, on the brink of a vast fortune, dozing.

'Wake up!' he shouted. 'The selling has begun.' Nomura groaned and rolled over to go back to sleep. Within days, the great bull market of 1906 became the great bear market of 1907, one of the most dramatic declines in the history of the Japanese stockmarket, comparable to the collapse of the St Petersburg exchange in 1917 and of the Shanghai stockmarket in 1949. In the twelve days from the peak of 19 January 1907 to the end of the month, the market shed one third of its value. By the end of 1907 the selling bloodbath had reduced the market's value by 88 per cent. The final reading on the index at the end of the year was a mere ninety-two, down from 774.

Nomura made three million yen — the equivalent of $60 million in current real terms. He became a legend.

★

To laugh often and much;
To win the respect of intelligent people
and the affection of children;
To earn the appreciation of honest critics
and endure the betrayal of false friends;
To appreciate beauty;
To find the best in others;
To leave the world a bit better,
whether by a healthy child, a garden
patch or a redeemed social condition;
To know even one life has breathed
easier because you have lived;
This is to have succeeded.
— 'What Is Success?' *by Ralph Waldo Emerson*

2 Leader of the Pack

How to Lead

Until fairly recently, it was popular to decry the value and contribution of leadership. Broad economic, sociological or organizational factors determined whether an enterprise prospered. A well-organized committee structure was seen as far more important than the quality of leadership. Economic turbulence and industrial change over the last twenty years has laid this myth to rest – for the present at least. Leaders make a crucial contribution to business success.

Leaders also take responsibility. This acceptance is wedded to a determination to share credit and accept blame. Smiles and patience in the face of adversity and pig-headed colleagues are more powerful tools than tantrums and haste. Resilience and the associated mental and physical toughness are part of the mix that distinguishes the leader from the led. Developing these characteristics is not easy. It calls for a high degree of self-discipline and application. John Adair draws out the dilemma facing leaders when he juxtaposes the willingness of leaders to accept responsibility and take risks with the commitment to give credit to others. They've taken the pain but must deny themselves the glory.

This is, of course, only part of the story. Leaders get ahead by thinking in the long term. The credit given to others motivates them to try harder. It binds others to them in a shared mission. Their own honour comes with long-term and deep-rooted success.

★

If, in order to succeed in an enterprise,
I were obliged to choose between fifty deer commanded by a lion,
and fifty lions commanded by a deer, I should consider myself
more certain of success with the first group than with the second.
– *Saint Vincent de Paul*

PATIENCE

Saint Vincent de Paul might have sympathized with the view of the British Army once expressed by the German General Staff – 'lions led by donkeys'. He would probably also have agreed with Charles Handy's 'leader's prayer' – especially its emphasis on patience, understanding, tolerance and that much neglected but powerful leadership tool, the smile. This emphasis on the needs of others is a constant feature of writings about successful leaders.

Understanding Organizations
by Charles Handy

A leader's prayer

Dear Lord, help me to become the kind of leader my management would like to have me be. Give me the mysterious something which will enable me at all times satisfactorily to explain policies, rules, regulations and procedures to my workers even when they have never been explained to me.

Help me to teach and to train the uninterested and dim-witted without ever losing my patience or my temper.

Give me that love for my fellow men which passeth all understanding so that I may lead the recalcitrant, obstinate, no-good worker into the paths of righteousness by my own example, and by soft persuading remonstrance, instead of busting him on the nose.

Instil into my inner-being tranquillity and peace of mind that no longer will I wake from my restless sleep in the middle of the night crying out 'What has the boss got that I haven't got and how did he get it?'

Teach me to smile if it kills me.

Make me a better leader of men by helping develop larger and greater qualities of understanding, tolerance, sympathy, wisdom, perspective, equanimity, mind-reading and second-sight.

And when, Dear Lord, Thou has helped me to achieve the high pinnacle my management has prescribed for me and when I shall have become the paragon of all supervisory virtues in this earthly world, Dear Lord, move over. Amen.

★

... men must either be pampered or crushed,
because they can get revenge for small injuries
but not for grievous ones.
— The Prince *by Niccolo Machiavelli*

★

Queen Victoria's Little Wars
by Byron Farwell

Although there had been several minor fights in 1806 and 1814, the first employment of British troops against the Ashanti warriors came in 1823 when Sir Charles Macarthy, the British governor at Cape Coast Castle, launched a punitive expedition against them. When the two armies came close, Sir Charles ordered the band to play 'God Save the King' while he stood to attention in the jungle, confidently expecting the Ashantis to join him. Instead they attacked, and Sir Charles's West Indian regiment and Fanti allies were soundly defeated. Sir Charles was killed and his skull taken to Kumasi where in future it was displayed annually at the Yam festival.

★

The most important quality in a leader is that
of being acknowledged as such. All leaders whose fitness
is questioned are clearly lacking in force.
— The Art of Living *by Andre Maurois*

PERFORMANCE

Sir Charles Macarthy's troops would no doubt have wished that he had listened more and postured less. Position is less important than performance when action is needed today, and the willingness of others to follow is more important than the desire to lead. Robert Townsend attacks the bureaucracies that have proliferated in so many companies. According to him, the pursuit of power and position dulls the senses and distracts people from the purpose of their efforts.

Further Up the Organisation
by Robert Townsend

True leadership must be for the benefit of the followers, not the enrichment of the leaders. In combat, officers eat last.

Most people in big companies today are administered, not led. They are treated as personnel, not people.

Something is happening to our country. We aren't producing leaders like we used to. A new chief executive officer today, exhausted by the climb to the peak, falls down on the mountaintop and goes to sleep.

Where are our corporate Ethan Allens and John Hancocks and Nathanael Greenes, to say nothing of our George Washingtons, Ben Franklins, and Thomas Jeffersons? If we had to get the modern equivalent of our Founding Fathers together today, the first thing they'd do would be to hire Cresap, McCormick, and Paget to write the Constitution for them.

I'm afraid leadership is becoming a lost art:

Most hierarchies are nowadays so cumbered with rules and traditions, and so bound in by public laws, that even high employees do not have to lead anyone anywhere, in the sense of pointing out the direction and setting the pace. They simply follow

precedents, obey regulations, and move at the head of the crowd. Such employees *lead* only in the sense that *the carved wooden figurehead leads the ship*.
(From *The Peter Principle* by Laurence J. Peter.)

How do you spot a leader? They come in all ages, shapes, sizes and conditions. Some are poor administrators, some are not overly bright. One clue: since most people per se are mediocre, the true leader can be recognized because, somehow or other, his people consistently turn in superior performances.

John Adair has probably done more to advance the study of leadership in Britain recently than any other individual. The way he structures his course on leadership is at one with Townsend's emphasis. Adair makes 'We' the most important word and 'I' the least important. This is in sharp contrast to the way many aspirant leaders see their role.

A Short Course on Leadership
The six most important words . . . 'I admit I made a mistake.'
The five most important words . . . 'I am proud of you.'
The four most important words . . . 'What is your opinion?'
The three most important words . . . 'If you please.'
The two most important words . . . 'Thank you.'
The one most important word . . . 'We.'
And the least most important word . . . 'I'.
– Effective Leadership *by John Adair*

QUALITIES

Golzen and Garner move beyond Adair's vision of the leaders to explore the relationship between leaders and managers. Their research into the common features of the background and attitudes of successful leader-managers allows them to draw out common elements. In the course of this analysis they place special emphasis on the ability of leader-managers to get things done and sustain this effort over time. They have, in Newbern's words, learned to 'make things happen'.

Smart Moves
by Godfrey Golzen & Andrew Garner

Managers and leaders

The single quality that is most generally identified as being necessary for those who want to get to the top is that of 'leadership'. But what is it that differentiates leaders from managers? And is there any real difference between them? The American management writer, Warren Bennis, has provided a definition of the distinction which is widely accepted. Managers, he says, do right things. Leaders do things right. In other

'I thought it would be a nice gesture to include a member of staff.'

words, managers are concerned with efficiently marshalling the physical resources of the organization. Leaders have the gift of inspiring people with a vision of the direction in which the organization, or even just their bit of the organization is going.

In reality management needs a bit of both. Even so-called charismatic leaders, who involve themselves very little in the day-to-day business of management, need good commercial judgement and the ability to build teams if they are to succeed. Hitler, for instance, is often picked out by managers as having been a good leader, leaving out the ethics of his regime. But he failed because he substituted hunches for work and because he lacked judgement.

Rather than talk about leaders and managers, one should therefore talk about managerial leaders. And although their characteristics are potentially almost endless, because success is also related to circumstances, there are some themes which run in common. Predicting success is a matter of looking at yourself and your life and career paths to date, and seeing how many of them have emerged in your case.

- High parental expectations.
- Early experiences of leadership.
- Ability to have – and communicate – clear objectives.
- Ability to take risks that come off.
- Decisiveness.
- Autonomy.
- Psychological and physical stamina.
- Ability to pick people.
- Ability to recognize your own strengths and weaknesses.

★

John Newbern's Law
People can be divided into three groups:
those who make things happen,
those who watch things happen,
and those who ask, 'What happened?'

STAMINA

John Harvey-Jones highlights the demands placed on the leaders themselves. Physical toughness and the ability to cope with these demands are pre-conditions for survival at the top. Leaders will also often be sustained by an ability to recognize why they are imposing these demands on themselves.

Making It Happen
by John Harvey-Jones

I have often said that the prime characteristic that I have detected in top leaders is mental and physical toughness. There is no doubt that these jobs are immensely demanding of time, concentration, sheer grinding brain power, and the ability to live an intrinsically unhealthy existence with some sort of control. The hours are, of necessity, very long, and one's body is continuously exposed to cruel punishment, not of the sort that toughens the muscles and develops strength, but rather of the sort that just places demands, without producing the increased ability to cope with them. Over the years I have only met one person who appeared totally impervious to jet lag. A life where you are never out of an aeroplane for more than a few days at a time is not a healthy one. It throws one's biological mechanisms into continual turmoil. Even if you are a man of the strongest possible character, and able to resist good food and drink, you are still almost certainly faced with the problems of entertaining at least twice a day, and now, with the fashion for working breakfasts, possibly three times a day. Most of your life is spent indoors, and you start early, and finish late. Physical exercise has to be sought as a matter of deliberation. It does not, so to speak, come packaged as a part of the job. When you get home at weekends, you find that your clock and your family's clocks are out of kilter. You have spent your whole week wining and dining, and dashing from here to there. They have been looking forward to the weekend as an opportunity to go out to entertain, and generally to live it up a little. All in all, if one sought to design a life style which was destructive of the individual, the way that business has structured itself would seem to be almost ideal!

For some prospective leaders the twin notions of sacrifice or denial on the part of leaders and support and recognition of the 'followers' defeats the entire purpose of seeking leadership. Lao-Tzu's emphasis on the leader stepping aside so that others can say, 'We did this ourselves,' highlights the distinction between leadership and vanity.

Keeping a low profile
A leader is best when people barely know that he exists;
not so good when people obey and acclaim him; worst
when they despise him. 'Fail to honour people, and they
fail to honour you.' But of a good leader who talks little,
when his work is done, his aim fulfilled, they will all say,
'We did this ourselves.'
— Lao-Tzu

PLANNING

Golzen and Garner explore the steps individuals who want to become leaders ought to follow. Their approach links the three P's of personal development in a structured approach. The three P's are Planning, Performance and People. Planning spells out both goals and the means to achieve them. Performance measures the real achievements in terms of business development while People indicates the value that individuals and groups bring to a task.

Smart Moves
by Godfrey Golzen & Andrew Garner

Business objectives over a 3–5 year period. Career objectives: where you would like to be in 3–5 years' time, in terms of function, level, industry, location, people you want to work with and the kind of experience you want to obtain. Goals are neither abstract nor absolute, but related to individual needs and, in broad terms, aspirations.

Business history. Career progression so far, patterns of achievement and personal satisfaction. Do these indicate that your objectives are realistic?

The background of the management team. Personal experience, responsibilities and where you need further development to reach your goals, either through formal training or additional experience.

The market for the business. The anticipated state of the job market over 3–5 years for existing personal skills, qualifications and experience by functions, type of business and geographical area. Are there any economic or technical changes emerging which might affect things positively or otherwise?

Products. What are the *doing* and *being* 'products' that you have to offer? Will they meet needs over a 3–5 year period? What adaptations, training and further development are required? What products do you definitely not have that are also beyond your reach, for example verbal or numerical skills of a higher order, or career anchors that are very firmly set? Do these factors matter in relation to your objectives?

Pricing. What are your reward aims and needs? Are they realistic? How flexible can you afford to be?

Suppliers. Can these various objectives of material reward, career development and broad personal ambition be met by existing 'suppliers' – in this case current employers and/or other providers of job opportunities? What specific action needs to be taken to ensure that suppliers are in place and able to deliver? You may end up being your own supplier – self-employed, running your own business.

Physical resources. Do you have what it takes, in terms of physical health and psychological stamina, to reach the objectives you have set yourself? Do you have the financial resources for self-employment or self-development; for example, can you take a year off to do an MBA? Or are you enough of a sticker to do it part time?

Contingency plans. Do you have a viable, personally satisfactory fall-back position, if you cannot reach your first objectives or cannot get the tools to do so? Particularly in the later stages of a career, it is important to have other things you can do, options and interests that can be developed.

CONTROL

The type of thoughtful approach to leadership development described by Golzen and Garner is an integral part of a leader's attempt to get control of situations. Warren Bennis, one of the most successful recent university leaders and public administrators in the USA, shows how easy it is to lose control and let circumstances dictate events. In effect, activity is confused with action. Recognizing this and taking steps to reverse the trend is, perhaps, the first step towards becoming an effective manager and a genuine leader.

The latter ability is central to Tom Peters' notion that leadership is increasingly important as firms try to impose themselves on increasingly complex, changing and chaotic markets. He makes one of the most basic leadership development points when he says that people pay far more attention to actions than words.

Warren Bennis,
while president of the University of Cincinnati

My moment of truth came toward the end of my first ten months. It was one of those nights in the office. The clock was moving toward four in the morning, and I was still not through with the incredible mass of paper stacked before me. I was bone weary and soul weary, and I found myself muttering, 'Either I can't manage this place, or it's unmanageable.' I reached for my calendar and ran my eyes down each hour, half-hour, quarter-hour to see where my time had gone that day, the day before, the month before. . . . My discovery was this: I had become the victim of a vast, amorphous, unwitting, unconscious conspiracy to prevent me from doing anything whatever to change the university's status quo.

★

Thriving on Chaos
by Tom Peters

In these uncertain times, when the need to accelerate the pace of change is paramount, we must:

- Lead, as never before, by personal example – in particular, calling attention to the new by means of our primary leadership tool: our calendars; that is, the way we spend our time.
- Reinforce attention to the new direction by the second most powerful day-to-day leadership tool – promotion decisions.
- Understand the power of our smallest actions: amidst uncertainty, when people are grasping at straws in an effort to understand the topsy-turvy world about them, their symbolic significance is monumental.

People in organizations are all boss-watchers, especially when external conditions are ambiguous. For better or worse, what you spend your *time* on (not what you sermonize about) will become the organization's preoccupation. Likewise, the proactive use of symbols, such as the sorts of stories you tell and the people you invite to meetings, sends powerful signals to the organization about what's important. The final confirmation of 'what really counts around here,' when things are changing, is who gets promoted – risk-takers and harbingers of the new, or 'the same old crowd'.

★

Wain's Sixth Conclusion
**Bosses are so busy delegating jobs,
they have no time to do any work.**

Sometimes the inconsistencies seen by subordinates are in the eye of the beholder. Leaders must take many things into account and look at issues from several perspectives before taking action. This balancing act was once used by Sir Monty Finneston to define the manager's special skill as being able to juggle three balls in the air with one hand while covering two more with another hand. One hopes that this metaphor will change in today's equal opportunity environment. John Sculley places special emphasis on this need by leaders to look at situations from different perspectives.

Odyssey: From Pepsi to Apple
by John Sculley

Explore external viewpoints

As a leader you need constantly to be able to shift your perspective to see the business from different points of view. A product view, a finance view, a manufacturing view, a sales view, a people view. You also need to gauge what's going on with some external reference points. Listening to outside constituencies and keeping them informed as to what you are doing is imperative. Your suppliers, customers, and others will give you a different perspective with which to compare your inside information. It's not possible to communicate with the outside world too much – even when you may believe it's a time to cut off all your external contacts.

PERSPECTIVE

Perspective is important in managing relationships with all colleagues. It gains its greatest value when the leader has sufficient credibility with subordinates for them to suspend judgement. Bill Scott places the building of credibility at the heart of the leadership process. Sculley shows how this credibility can lend distance to the perspective and continually reinforce the leader's esteem. But, as Wain points out, pride comes before a fall.

Into Profit
by Bill Scott

The importance of your leadership

The most important factor in countering these problems and re-motivating your staff is going to be you yourself. It is going to hinge on your leadership and on the example you set to everyone in the company.

The key to providing leadership in this situation lies in a number of very basic points:

- Help people to believe in success.
- Identify closely with them.
- Be visible and keep smiling.
- Establish your own credibility.

You must believe that you are going to succeed and you must make the people in the company believe that with your leadership you will achieve success together. Unless it is your natural style, avoid the 'action man' role. Resist, for example, the temptation to fire some managers simply to prove that you are not afraid to take drastic action. You may very well need to prune the dead wood out of your management team, but do it at the right time and for the right reasons. Avoid also the politician's gimmicks, like a programme for the 'the first 100 days'; your critical time-scale may in real life be shorter, or longer, than that.

★

Odyssey: From Pepsi to Apple
by John Sculley

When Napoleon Bonaparte wanted to extend the reach of his armies, he believed he should allow them to march in the heat of the summer. So strong were the sun's rays that he proposed lining the major roads in France with shaded trees.

One of his ministers responded in shocked amazement: 'But Emperor Napoleon, they will take thirty years to grow!'

Replied the adventurer who created a French empire: 'Then we don't have a moment to waste!'

★

Wain's First Conclusion
**He who gets too big for his britches
gets exposed in the end.**

*'I have a challenging assignment for you, Robson!
I want you to go out and find another job.'*

3 It's Getting Better All the Time

How to Be an Outstanding Manager

One of the pleasures of listening to Sir John Harvey-Jones speak is to get a sense of his delight in self development. He clearly enjoys learning and finding how to improve the way in which he manages his work and his life. This determination to learn and improve is a common characteristic of successful firms and effective managers.

The determination to learn and improve shows itself in a host of ways. Tom Peters probably identifies the most basic when he emphasises the willingness to 'ask dumb questions'. This has value on several levels. The most fundamental is acknowledging a need to know and a refusal to put fear, vanity or any other emotions or attitudes before a responsibility to manage better. Questioning, trying to get things right, marks out those managers who take their responsibilities seriously from those who cannot make the switch from administration to management. Good managers realize that the difference between them and others in the business lies in the transition they have made from completing jobs and tasks themselves to 'getting things done through others'. Whatever the manager achieves has a multiplier effect. If she or he gets it right, others will get it right. If she or he screws it up, others will screw it up.

★

Heller's Law
The first myth of management is that it exists.

FIRST PRINCIPLES

There is widespread debate about the first principles of management. For some, like Sir John Harvey-Jones, the emphasis is on personal style and the ability to wed this style to the needs of particular situations and circumstances. Kenneth Blanchard and Spencer Johnson highlight the importance of a specific portfolio of skills, usually linked with personal productivity and working with others. Despite the importance of style, it is hard to see any personal style which cannot be improved by a proper sense of personal discipline and a willingness to say 'thank you'.

'Langford, will you stop quoting Sir John Harvey-Jones!'

Making It Happen
by John Harvey-Jones

I find myself intolerant of management books that seek to prescribe exactly 'how it should be done'. My own experience shows that there are many different ways of achieving one's aims and many different ways of leading an industrial company. I have worked with leaders whose style is so totally different to my own that I have found it incomprehensible that they achieve results, but nevertheless they do. Each one of us has to develop our own style, and our own approach, using such skills and personal qualities as we have inherited. . . . My own experience of trying to teach and train managers is that it is extremely difficult to teach grown-up people anything. It is, however, relatively easy to create conditions under which people will teach themselves. Indeed most people wish to improve their own performance and are eager to do so. That is why there are so many books on management published and that is why I have read practically all of them. As I said earlier, too many make impossible promises and claims for no one can manage or lead in someone else's clothes. What each of us does over a long period of trial and error is to acquire a set of tools with which we are comfortable and which we can apply in different ways to the myriad problems which we need to solve.

★

From The One Minute Manager
by Kenneth Blanchard & Spencer Johnson

Drucker links the notion of core personal skills outlined by Blanchard and Johnson on the previous page to a 'rule of thumb' about the ways managers look at situations. His 'well-tried and tested approaches' give managers a framework which they can apply to a host of situations almost regardless of their personal style. Mintzberg sees this extension of the manager's skills in handling specific tasks as posing a major problem for long-term organizational effectiveness. He worries that the ability – even the desire – to display a new set of skills can get in the way of real contributions to the enterprise.

Managing for Results
by Peter Drucker

To make business effective the executive has available three well-tried and tested approaches:

1 He can start with a model of the 'ideal business' which would produce maximum results from the available markets and knowledge – or at least those results that, over a long period, are likely to be most favourable.
2 He can try to maximize opportunities by focusing the available resources on the most attractive possibilities and devoting them to obtaining the greatest possible results.
3 He can maximize resources so that those opportunities are found – if not created – that endow the available high-quality resources with the greatest possible impact.

★

'Professional management' is the great invention
of this century, an invention that produced
gains in organizational *efficiency* so great that
it eventually destroyed organizational *effectiveness*.
– Mintzberg on Management *by Henry Mintzberg*

QUESTIONS

There is a continuing notion of the manager as technical expert. Experts know the answers, so questions are irrelevant. But listening to questions, comments and concerns is one of the most important skills of the effective manager. Tom Peters returns to basics when he highlights the need to ask questions if you do not understand, even when it makes you look 'dumb'. The attempt to carry on regardless is probably the biggest single contribution to the continued relevance of Murphy's Laws.

Launegayer's Observation
**Asking dumb questions is easier
than correcting dumb mistakes.**

★

Thriving on Chaos
by Tom Peters

I was blessed early in my consulting career at McKinsey & Company. My first boss, Allen Puckett, is one of the smartest people I know. He was smart enough and comfortable enough with himself to ask really elementary (some would say dumb) questions.

He'd be with an oil executive from Getty who was paying us a bundle to be there. The fellow would, unselfconsciously, be talking a private language: rigs, wildcatters, landsmen, scouts, stepouts, tertiary recovery. Whenever Allen would hear a word he didn't understand, he'd ask. 'What's tertiary recovery?' he'd say. 'Stepouts?' The rest of us were scared stiff; we assumed that since we were being paid an exorbitant fee, we shouldn't ask dumb questions. But the result was we'd lose 90 per cent of the strategic value of the interview because we were afraid to display our ignorance by asking, 'What's a barrel of oil?'

Mostly, it's the 'dumb,' elementary questions, followed up by a dozen even more elementary questions, that yield the pay dirt. 'Why in the heck does this form go *there* next?' and 'Who has to sign it?' are probably the two most vital questions when it comes to discussing the reason a firm is slow to act on something. 'Experts' are those who don't need to bother with elementary questions anymore – thus, they fail to 'bother' with the true sources of bottlenecks, buried deep in the habitual routines of the firm, labelled 'we've always done it that way.'

★

Murphy's Seventh Law
Left to themselves, things tend to go from bad to worse.

Murphy's Eighth Law
If everything seems to be going well,
you have obviously overlooked something.

LISTENING

Mark McCormack has built his International Management Group into a billion-dollar sports company by spotting trends and opportunities. It is his ability to identify talent that holds the key to this success. In all his books, he highlights the importance of listening and learning from others: you hear with your ears open, not your mouth. McCormack's success is closely linked with his skill in networking and building strong relations.

What They Don't Teach You at Harvard Business School
by Mark McCormack

Listen aggressively

The ability to listen, really to hear what someone is saying, has far greater business implications, of course, than simply gaining insight into people. In selling, for instance, there is probably no greater asset. But the bottom line is that almost any business situation will be handled differently, and with different results, by someone who is listening and someone who isn't.

When I was preparing to write this book I asked a number of my business friends, several of them chairmen of companies, what business advice they would give if they were writing it. Almost without exception, and often at the top of their lists, they said, 'Learn to be a good listener.'

Observe aggressively

I will often fly great distances to meet someone face-to-face, even when I can say much of what needs to be said over the phone. If it's important, or if it's a relationship that may be long-term, I want to form impressions based on what I observe even more than on what I hear. After all, the impression you have from meeting someone in person is often quite different from that formed in speaking over the phone.

Observation is an aggressive act. People are constantly revealing themselves in ways that will go unnoticed unless you are aggressively involved in noticing them.

THINKING

These skills seldom come naturally or easily. Employing a core portfolio of personal disciplines can provide the time to think as well as the opportunity to build links and develop relationships. Thinking skills, or at least the skill to think smarter than rivals, is perhaps the most neglected management skill. But, as Drucker points out, thinking smarter can produce success against even the most entrenched rivals. Sloan outflanked Ford and designed a management system which provided fifty years of dominance for General Motors.

Enterprise
by Tom Cannon

'*Get into the habit of writing things down.*' This is the fundamental premise of most attempts to improve the quality of analysis. . . . Follow the 'describe what you know; what you don't know; and what you need to know' advice given to aspiring journalists. The essential disciplines lie in:

● taking time to think
● thinking about the issue(s) first
● arriving at solutions only after the issue is understood
● building up a word picture of the situation.

The relationship between analysis and conclusion is especially important. It takes very little skill to find a justification for virtually any choice or decision. To avoid this precipitous choice or action requires a prior analysis which incorporates as much relevant information as possible even if the material gathered is uncomfortable because it does not fit in with the preconceived ideas or assumptions. Mistakes are better made on a sheet of paper than in a workplace.

★

Cole's First Rule
**The human mind is like a parachute –
it functions best when it is open.**

★

Managing for Results
by Peter Drucker

Sloan rightly believed that unchallenged success was dangerous, and so provided each of his five makes with at least one strong challenger from within the family.

This design made General Motors within five years both the dominant American automobile manufacturer and by far the most profitable one. And when Ford itself hit the comeback trail after World War II, it deliberately adopted the Sloan design and imported executives from General Motors who had been reared in the Sloan concept and strategy.

For the early 1920s, Sloan's design was radical – so radical indeed that it was quite a few years before his associates at General Motors accepted it. It violated all the then 'known facts'. Instead of dividing the potential customers sharply into a mass-market wanting uniform automobiles at the lowest possible price, and a class-market with low volume and high prices, Sloan saw the customers as essentially homogeneous, demanding mass-production but also performance, low price and easy sale of a used car as well as an annual model change, comfort and styling.

Sloan did not try to dislodge Ford by doing just as well, nor even by doing better. He never considered doing again what Ford had done before; that is, building the cheapest, standardized, changeless car. Instead, he made the Model T obsolete through something which neither Ford (nor anyone else) could possibly produce: the one-year-old, secondhand car. It had been the new car only one year earlier. As 'transportation' it could easily compete with the Model T. It had the appearance, styling and performance of the high-priced cars, but was cheaper even than the Model T.

★

I keep six honest serving men
(They taught me all I knew);
Their names are *What* and *Why* and *When*,
And *How* and *Where* and *Who*.
– *Rudyard Kipling*

GROUP-THINK

Sometimes smart managers show their thinking skills by challenging accepted ideas and the consensus of the group.

Charles Handy draws on the work of US political scientists to outline the dangers of 'group-think' and the need for some people to challenge accepted ideas. President Kennedy's problems have been repeated in boardrooms across the world as old models are retained in the face of innovation or new rivals are discounted because of cosy stereotypes. Sometimes it is necessary to throw conventional models of inquiry out of the window and seek new ways of looking at situations.

Understanding Organizations
by Charles Handy

'How could we have been so stupid?' asked President John F. Kennedy, after he and a group of close advisers had blundered into the Bay of Pigs invasion.

Stupidity was certainly not the explanation. The group who made the decision was one of the greatest collections of intellectual talent in the history of American government. Irving Janis describes the blunder as a result of 'group-think'.

Group-think occurs when too high a price is placed on the harmony and morale of the group, so that loyalty to the group's previous policies, or to the group consensus, overrides the conscience of each member. 'Concurrence-seeking' drives out the realistic appraisal of alternatives. No bickering or conflict is allowed to spoil the cosy 'we-feeling' of the group. Thus it is that even the cleverest, most high-minded and well-intentioned of people can get into a blind spot. Janis identifies eight symptoms:

1 *Invulnerability*. Cohesive groups become over-optimistic and can take extraordinary risks without realizing the dangers, mainly because there is no discordant warning voice.
2 *Rationale*. Cohesive groups are quick to find rationalizations to explain away evidence that does not fit their policies.

3 *Morality.* There is a tendency to be blind to the moral or ethical implications of a policy. 'How could so many good men be wicked?' is the feeling.
4 *Stereotypes.* Victims of group-think quickly get into the habit of stereotyping their enemies or other people and do not notice discordant evidence.
5 *Pressure.* If anyone starts to voice doubts the group exerts subtle pressures to keep him quiet: he is allowed to express doubts but not to press them.
6 *Self-censorship.* Members of the group are careful not to discuss their feelings or their doubts outside the group, in order not to disturb the group cosiness.
7 *Unanimity.* Unanimity is important so, once a decision has been reached, any divergent views are carefully screened out in people's minds.
8 *Mindguards.* Victims of group-think set themselves up as bodyguards to the decision. 'He needs all the support we can give him. The doctrine of collective responsibility is invoked to stifle dissent outside the group.

The result of group-think is that the group looks at too few alternatives, is insensitive to the risks in its favourite strategy, finds it hard to rethink a strategy that is failing and becomes very selective in the sort of facts it sees and asks for.

Group-think is unfortunately most rife at the top and centre of organizations where the need for 'keeping things close' seems more important. Such groups must actively encourage self-criticism, the search for more alternatives, the introduction of outside ideas and evaluation wherever possible, and a positive response to conflicting evidence. One way of avoiding group-think in the boardroom is the growing use of non-executive directors, for small groups can get *too* cohesive to be effective.

Kennedy learnt his lesson. The Missile Crisis was handled differently, with a more diffuse group, more outside ideas, more testing of alternatives and more sensitivity to conflicting data.

ORGANISING

Edison once commented that invention was one per cent inspiration and ninety-nine per cent perspiration. Even a creative entrepreneur like McCormack organizes his work around a set of basic personal disciplines. These give him the time and space to concentrate on other issues. Ray Kroc and John Sculley emphasize different but closely related aspects of this need to organize to produce results, while the extract from Charles Handy emphasizes the need to deploy different talents to deal with varying issues.

What They Don't Teach You at Harvard Business School
by Mark McCormack

I have never known a successful person in business who didn't operate from some personal organizational system.

There are two points about the way I organize myself which have an almost universal application.

First, *write it down*. Write it down anywhere, shirt-sleeves if necessary, but write it down. This allows you to free your mind for other things. But more important, *it means you are going to do it.* Writing something down is a commitment. Once you have performed this physical act you have provided the momentum for getting something done. The agony of carrying over an item and the ecstasy that comes with crossing it off will provide further incentive.

Second, *organize for the next day at the end of the previous day.* This is what gives me peace of mind at night, a feeling that I am on top of things, and a real excitement about coming into work the next morning. Simply by arranging the next day – defining on paper what I want to accomplish – I feel that I have a head start.

★

Nothing in the world can take the place of persistence.
Talent will not; nothing is more common than
unsuccessful men with talent. Genius will not;
unrewarded genius is almost a proverb. Education will
not; the world is full of educated derelicts. Persistence
and determination alone are omnipotent.
– *Ray Kroc: founder and for many years
Chairman of McDonald's*

★

At Pepsi, we lived for the smallest details.
– Odyssey: From Pepsi to Apple *by John Sculley*

★

The Age of Unreason
by Charles Handy

We need more talents than the intellect, important though that is. Talent, we know, has many faces. So does intelligence. Howard Gardner, a professor at the Harvard School of Education, took the trouble to classify seven different types of intelligence which, he claims, we can actually measure. Based on his analysis, but stretching it a little, we can in a common-sense way recognize some distinct sorts of intelligence or talent in people, even at a young age.

1 *Analytical intelligence*
The sort we measure in IQ tests and in most examinations.
2 *Pattern intelligence*
The ability to see patterns in things and to create patterns. Mathematicians, artists, computer programmers often have this intelligence to a high degree. (It is important to realize that the talents are not connected or correlated. It is possible to be very intelligent in a pattern sense and to fail all conventional exams.)
3 *Musical intelligence*
Some musicians, pop stars, for example, are analytically clever but many are not. Musically intelligent they undoubtedly are.
4 *Physical intelligence*
Swimmers, footballers, sports stars of all sorts have this talent in abundance – it is no guarantee of the other talents.
5 *Practical intelligence*
The sort of intelligence that can take a television to bits, put it together again without instructions, but might not be able to spell the names of the parts.
6 *Intra-personal intelligence*
The person, often the quiet one, who is in tune with feelings, their own and others, the poets and the counsellors.
7 *Inter-personal intelligence*
The ability to get on with other people, to get things done with and through others. It is the skill that managers have to have, in addition to one or other of the first two types.

★

Hood's Warning
Be sure the brain is engaged before putting the mouth in gear.

WINNING WAYS

The purpose of organizing is to get the best from yourself and others. The latter means understanding the needs and potential of those with whom we work. Far too often, managers apply the same solution regardless of circumstances. Thomas Horton and Peter Reid used their experiences as Chief Executive of the American Management Association and as a journalist, respectively, to build a portfolio of approaches to different types of managers based on their current performance.

Beyond the Trust Gap
by Thomas Horton & Peter Reid

Low-producing managers

- Rigidly imposed production goals on their subordinates.
- Directed employee behaviour by minutely organizing each job, exactly prescribing methods, and setting rigid standards.
- Often tried to cajole employees into working harder with artificial 'human relations' techniques, tried to turn work into a game with contests and other manipulative devices, or used the threat of dismissal or demotion as their main motivating device.
- Placed more importance on controlling the *conduct* of their subordinates than on controlling the *results* achieved.

High-producing managers

- Supported the 'pyschological advantage' of their subordinates by letting them do their work in their own way.
- Set general goals and standards.
- Expected their subordinates to do their work effectively and used measurements largely to find out where there were problems they could help resolve.

- Were more interested in controlling the *results* achieved by their subordinates than in controlling their *conduct*.

Companies must face the fact that some managers will *never* make the adjustment from one managerial style to the other.

Horton and Reid are clear that using this portfolio is not the same as being unsure or unclear about goals or approaches. Robert Townsend argues strongly that choices must be made even when a comfortable compromise seems possible.

Further Up the Organisation
by Robert Townsend

Compromise is usually bad. It should be a last resort. If two departments or divisions have a problem they can't solve and it comes up to you, listen to both sides and then, unlike Solomon, pick one or the other. This places solid accountability on the winner to make it work.

Condition your people to avoid compromise. Teach them to win some battles, lose others gracefully. Work on the people who try to win them all. For the sake of the organization, others must have a fair share of victories.

When you give in, give in all the way. And when you win, try to win all the way so the responsibility to make it work rests squarely on you.

★

Wain's Second Conclusion
**Staying afloat in management is easier
if you don't make big waves.**

EFFECTIVENESS

In part, Townsend's view reflects his determination to force his staff at Avis to make hard choices and concentrate on producing the best, not the easiest, outcome. He links this closely with the search for greater managerial effectiveness. The distinction between effectiveness and efficiency is subject to close scrutiny in the work of Bill Reddin, one of the most influential writers on the way managers work in organizations.

Managerial Effectiveness
by William J. Reddin

There is only one realistic and unambiguous definition of managerial effectiveness. Effectiveness is the extent to which a manager achieves the output requirements of his position. This concept of managerial effectiveness is the central issue in management. It is the manager's job to be effective. It is his only job. Managerial effectiveness has to be defined in terms of output rather than input, by what a manager achieves rather than by what he does.

★

Peter's Corollaries
1 Incompetence knows no barriers of time or place.
2 Work is accomplished by those employees
who have not yet reached their level of incompetence.
3 If at first you don't succeed, try something else.

★

Effectiveness means:

Doing the right things *not* Doing things right
Avoiding recurrent difficulties *not* Solving specific problems
Optimising use *not* Safeguarding resources
Obtaining results *not* Following duties
Increasing returns *not* Lowering costs

Adapted from Managerial Effectiveness *by William J. Reddin*

The distinction between effectiveness and efficiency runs right through the work of W. Edwards Deming, the great US advocate of quality management. Deming was the classic 'prophet in his own land' until the 1980s. For thirty years, he had been working with some of the most successful Japanese firms as they established the production, management and quality systems which allowed them to dominate so much of world industry.

Deming Management at Work
by Mary Walton

The Fourteen Points

1 *Create constancy of purpose for improvement of product and service.* Dr Deming suggests a radical new definition of a company's role: rather than to make money, it is to stay in business and provide jobs through innovation, research, constant improvement and maintenance.

2 *Adopt the new philosophy.* Americans are too tolerant of poor workmanship and sullen service. We need a new religion in which mistakes and negativism are unacceptable.

3 *Cease dependence on mass inspection.* American firms typically inspect a product as it comes off the assembly line or at major stages along the way; defective products are either thrown out or reworked. Both practices are unnecessarily expensive. In effect, a company is paying workers to make defects and then to correct them. Quality comes not from inspection but from improvement of the process. With instruction, workers can be enlisted in this improvement.

4 *End the practice of awarding business on the price tag alone.* Purchasing departments customarily operate on orders to seek the lowest-priced vendor. Frequently, this leads to supplies of low quality. Instead, buyers should seek the best quality in a long-term relationship with a single supplier for any one item.

5 *Improve constantly and forever the system of production and service.* Improvement is not a one-time effort.

Management is obligated to continually look for ways to reduce waste and improve quality.

6 *Institute training.* Too often, workers have learned their job from another worker who was never trained properly. They are forced to follow unintelligible instructions. They can't do their jobs well because no one tells them how to do so.

7 *Institute leadership.* The job of a supervisor is not to tell people what to do nor to punish them but to lead. Leading consists of helping people do a better job and of learning by objective methods who is in need of individual help.

8 *Drive out fear.* Many employees are afraid to ask questions or to take a position, even when they do not understand what their job is or what is right or wrong. They will continue to do things the wrong way, or not do them at all. The economic losses from fear are appalling. To assure better quality and productivity, it is necessary that people feel secure.

9 *Break down barriers between staff areas.* Often a company's departments or units are competing with each other or have goals that conflict. They do not work as a team so they can solve or foresee problems. Worse, one department's goals may cause trouble for another.

10 *Eliminate slogans, exhortations and targets for the work force.* These never helped anybody do a good job. Let workers formulate their own slogans.

11 *Eliminate numerical quotas.* Quotas take into account only numbers, not quality or methods. They are usually a guarantee of inefficiency and high cost. A person, to hold a job, meets a quota at any cost, without regard to damage to his company.

12 *Remove barriers to pride of workmanship.* People are eager to do a good job and distressed when they cannot. Too often, misguided supervisors, faulty equipment and defective materials stand in the way of good performance. These barriers must be removed.

13 *Institute a vigorous programme of education and retraining.* Both management and the work force will have to be educated in the new methods, including teamwork and statistical techniques.

14 *Take action to accomplish the transformation.* It will require a special top management team with a plan of action to carry out the quality mission. Workers cannot do it on their own, nor can managers. A critical mass of people in the company must understand the Fourteen Points and the Seven Deadly Diseases. . . .

The Seven Deadly Diseases

1 *Lack of constancy of purpose.* A company that is without constancy of purpose has no long-range plans for staying in business. Management is insecure, and so are employees.

2 *Emphasis on short-term profits.* Looking to increase the quarterly dividend undermines quality and productivity.

3 *Evaluation by performance, merit rating or annual review of performance.* The effects of these are devastating – teamwork is destroyed, rivalry is nurtured. Performance ratings build fear and leave people bitter, despondent, beaten. They also encourage defection in the ranks of management.

4 *Mobility of management.* Job-hopping managers never understand the companies they work for and are never there long enough to follow through on long-term changes that are necessary for quality and productivity.

5 *Running a company on visible figures alone.* The most important figures are unknown and unknowable – the 'multiplier' effect of a happy customer, for example.

6 *Excessive medical costs for employee health care,* which increase the final costs of goods and services.

7 *Excessive costs of warranty,* fuelled by lawyers who work on the basis of contingency fees.

★

**Always reject an expenses claim with
a bottom line divisible by 5 or 10.**

CONTROLS

*Some of Dr Deming's followers in the quality revolution
present his work in terms of broad qualitative changes in
operations. In fact, he places a heavy emphasis on statistical
control techniques and management control. Similar confusion
can be seen in the external view of the disciplines taught at
Harvard Business School. The verbal and behaviour skills
employed in much case study analysis can blind observers to
the emphasis placed on effective controls and tightly specified
requirements.*

What They Really Teach You
at the Harvard Business School
by Francis J. Kelly & Heather M. Kelly

These four fundamental questions are examined from a variety
of managerial perspectives in Control:

1 How has the organization done in the past?
2 How will it do in the future?
3 How can management measure performance against its
   objectives and help ensure the organization's future
   success?
4 How should management communicate this performance
   to stakeholders, both inside and outside the organization?

★

What They Really Teach You
at the Harvard Business School
by Francis J. Kelly & Heather M. Kelly

Control checklist

These questions will help direct one's thinking about whether a company has effective management control and information systems in place.

1 Are there management controls, particularly budgeting systems, in place for each organizational unit?
2 Do managers have control over the variables in their budget for which they are responsible?
3 Are the budget objectives for each unit reasonable and are they designed to give people proper incentive to act in a manner that helps achieve the company's objectives?
4 Are the budget systems tied to the strategic planning and reward systems?
5 Are there systems in place for periodically measuring the performance of each segment of the business?
6 Do these measurement systems provide the most appropriate and meaningful information needed for managers to make sound business decisions?
7 Who's in charge of designing, implementing, and monitoring the appropriateness of the management control and information systems? Does that person have credibility and authority within the organization?
8 Does management effectively communicate its corporate performance to stakeholders?

★

**Management is the art of getting other people
to do all the work.**

4 Another Sleepless Night
Managing Time, Managing Stress, Managing Yourself

'*Managers are people too*' *should be the underlying premise of any guide to business success. Too often managers forget this simple principle when they are making demands on themselves and others. The most basic and most easily avoided barriers to success can often be found in poor self-awareness, bad time management and stress. Executives who can appraise the most complex sets of accounts, markets or technologies balk at the idea of self-assessment, even when doubts and worries gnaw at their confidence and esteem.*

These feelings are often strongest when time and other pressures produce a sense of inadequacy and powerlessness. The rules of time management (lists, blocking, prioritization, distinguishing between urgent and important, and delegation) are probably the best known, least applied features of management. That said, they are fundamental to getting ahead in business. Some of the best managers have become totally ruthless in their approach to their time. I wish that I had the courage to follow Dr Laurence Peter's simple principles or was willing to accept my waste bin as an integral part of my filing system. Successful time managers tend to see the attempt to manage their time as an ongoing battle. Some victories have to be won for any progress. You have to recognize the importance of time. Some structure is essential. You have to say **NO** *sometimes. Other victories get easier as skill and resulting authority increase.*

As Bill Shankly once said – 'I never had any education – so I had to use my brains.'

★

KNOW YOURSELF

O wad some power the giftie gie us
To see oursel's as others see us.
– *Robert Burns*

There is a school of management writing that talks about managers and management as if it involved beings with no existence outside their role as executives of this firm or that organization. At times they are pawns to be moved in one direction or another. At other times they are supermen and women, coping with chaos, reengineering their corporations or breaking through barriers of time and space. None of these images is true. Managers are people facing most of the stress of everyday life but with the task of leading others and building their firms to create wealth for communities. Coping with their work calls for the type of self-awareness identified in The Manager's Handbook, *as well as the kind of understanding of reality highlighted by David Clutterbuck in his piece which follows. His research into the factors that make managers successful has made him one of Britain's most authoritative business gurus.*

The Manager's Handbook
by Arthur Young

Who are you?

Self-knowledge is invaluable to anyone seriously intent on choosing the right life-path. If you, as a manager, don't know yourself, you will be led into making ill-advised decisions about your life and work from which it may be difficult or impossible to extricate yourself.

If you are not enjoying your job, look at situations in the past where you have enjoyed yourself and done well at something. The chances are that you have strayed away from your natural abilities and a move to recapture them will be rewarding for you and the company you work for.

Am I in the right job?

People's values and interests change. Every so often you should ask yourself the following questions to find out whether you are still satisfied with your job. There is no 'right' answer except the truthful one.

- Do you begin to feel anxious in the evening at the prospect of work the next day?
- Do you talk obsessively to your partner about your work or about a member of staff? Or are you unnaturally reticent about them?
- Do you find yourself working late regularly or not taking your lunch hour because you feel you need to impress or because you have been given, or taken on, too much work?
- Are you offhand or short-tempered with your subordinates or peer colleagues?
- Are you enjoying your job and clear about where it is taking you?
- Do you feel your boss is incompetent and that you could do his/her job just as well?
- Do you have pangs of envy when you hear your friends talk about their jobs? What do you envy? Their freedom? Responsibility? Opportunity to travel? Salary?
- Are you sick of being delegated to and not delegating?
- Do you feel run-down or stressed?
- Have you had to give up hobbies or interests because of work?

★

Wain's Eighth Conclusion
**You can tell some people aren't afraid of work
by the way they fight it.**

Makers of Management
by David Clutterbuck & Stuart Crainer

. . . in actually *forming* strategy, managers do the following:

- They manage stability, that is, they make sure that the strategies they have are pursued vigorously and that the implications are formally worked out. If they try to reassess strategy continuously they end up unable to implement anything.
- They detect discontinuity, that is, they look for changes that might make a serious difference to their business. Once again, intuition comes to the fore. 'The real challenge in crafting strategy lies in detecting the subtle discontinuities that may undermine a business in the future. And for that, there is no technique, no program, just a sharp mind in touch with the situation.'
- They know the business, not in an intellectual way, but by personal feel for what makes it tick.
- They manage patterns. When they detect beneficial patterns emerging, they intervene to help them take shape. This implies letting a large number of strategies germinate, then weeding periodically to allow the most promising room to grow.
- They reconcile change and continuity. They decide when to hold back a strategy whose time has not yet come, and when to let rip with new strategies.

Henry Mintzberg of Canada's McGill University is the enfant terrible of business academics. His work emphasizes the reality of the management job against the type of grand theory which seeks to portray the manager as a mixture of action man and Einstein. His early work identified the very short time-spans most managers can allocate to tasks before interruptions, new instructions or simply new pressures force them on. The manager's real task is to make judgements which lead to actions which produce results – often in spite of the organization which surrounds him.

Mintzberg on Management
by Henry Mintzberg

An irrational form of 'rationality' underlies our attraction to machine bureaucracy. Certain fields try to control words. The statisticians, for example, have tried to take over the word 'significant,' and in so doing may have reversed its meaning (since so much that proved 'statistically significant' turned out to be trivial). So too, the economists have tried to take over the word 'rational,' with much the same effect. As human beings, we must above all be 'rational,' meaning to emphasize a strictly logical, explicit, and analytical – basically linear – form of reasoning. Everything must be worked out in advance, ideally based on numerical calculation.

This notion of rationality really amounts to mental control – mind over matter – and to the 'rational' mind, mental control is the most important kind of control. And so organizations obsessed with control become organizations obsessed with this form of rationality.

To be in control in the machine bureaucracy means above all, to have it down on paper. A market is controlled if a high number appears next to the label 'market share'; quality is controlled if a low number appears next to 'defects'; work is controlled if its accomplishment has been duly ticked off on a sheet of paper; people are controlled if each is connected to a boss on an organigram; the whole system is controlled if everything that must happen is recorded in a document called a 'plan'. It matters not that the real world goes its own merry way, so long as the mind controls the records of that world on paper. We deal with the discrepancies that arise through a process known as 'creative accounting'!

How rational is this form of 'rationality'? If no other form of thinking existed short of the haphazard, of if any other form that did exist was demonstrably inferior, then it would appear to be rational.

In fact, however, there is another form of thinking. We have long sensed it, have even had labels for it, although it has only been in recent years, through the hard science of physiology, that we discovered it. It appears to have been hiding all along in the mute right hemisphere of the human brain. We still do not know much about it – our words for it, 'intuition' and 'judgment', just label our ignorance – except that it seems to be inaccessible to our conscious ('rational') minds and appears to be neither linear nor analytical in its workings. Processing seems to take place in parallel, in a more holistic manner, oriented to synthesis.

If to be rational really means to use the process that most effectively achieves your goals, then intuition, no matter how mysterious, has never been demonstrated to be any less rational than conventional formal 'rationality' – no one has ever proved it to be an inferior process. Of course, how could they? The concept of proof itself resides in conventional rationality. How can we allow 'rational' argument to prove or disprove the inferiority of a thought process that itself is beyond rationality? That would be like using black-and-white photography to study the colors of the rainbow.

If this is true, then machine bureaucracies, because they accept only the narrow form of rationality, must be considered irrational organizations. Such rationality has been their obsession since Frederick Taylor began his time and motion studies of factory workers a century ago. Taylor's purpose was to root out instinct, intuition, and judgment in favor of this narrow form of rationality. From the factory, this same orientation moved into the office, as 'rational' operations research techniques and formal information systems become popular after World War II. It then moved up the hierarchy, to culminate in the use of 'strategic planning' in the executive suite. Such 'rational' thinking has likewise dominated our business schools, which ostensibly train managers as if their brains had only one hemisphere. The old joke about MBA meaning 'management by analysis' is no joke at all.

Bear in mind what 'rationality' means in management, whether business, government, or the parapublic sector – it makes no difference. To rationalize almost inevitably means to cut, to reduce, to eliminate, not to integrate or grow or create. In effect, rationalizing is to the contemporary manager what bloodletting was to the medieval physician.

★

Sheetz's Ruminations
1 It's not whether you win or lose,
   but how you place the blame.
2 A friend in need is a friend to avoid.
3 You don't have to be a cannibal
   to get fed up with people.
4 To err is human; to forgive is against company policy.
5 When it comes to giving, some people stop at nothing.
6 The way some people find fault,
   you'd think there was a reward.
7 Those who think they know it all
   are very annoying to those who do.

TIME

Getting the best from yourself and others is an integral part of good management. This means using all available resources to their best advantage. One resource is available in equal measure to all managers. This is time. John Harvey-Jones knows better than most the types of pressures that deflect executives from the best use of the time available. Cutting waste is the first step towards getting control of this asset. It is a lesson which John Adair found many successful leaders learn early. His checklist highlights both the ease with which time can be wasted and the relatively simple disciplines involved in getting control. But schedules and structures are only the start. Mark McCormack gets his competitive edge by sticking to schedules and accepting that wishful thinking has never added hours to the day or shortened a journey.

Hoffman's Law of Conservation
Next to the dog, the wastebasket is man's best friend.

★

Making It Happen
by John Harvey-Jones

No amount of 'tricks of the trade' will avoid the need to set some sort of priority when allocating one's time. No matter how carefully and cleverly every moment of the day is utilized, and no matter how ingeniously staff, gadgetry, and the most modern devices are used to improve one's productivity, there will never be enough time to do everything that is asked of you. This is where you must set clear guidelines as to how your time is to be spent, and it is well worth while discussing the basis of these time allocations with your staff, and reviewing them from time to time. Some priorities are immutable. In my own case, in ICI, anything which had to do with customers, or customer relationships, took absolute priority over anything else. Any of our people in the world who wished me to appear to talk to customers, or to help them with a customer opportunity, or problem, always got an automatic priority. . . .

After a relatively simple problem of deciding one's first priorities you must then establish some sort of pecking order, and how you are going to allocate your time between internal and external matters, between showing the flag and troubleshooting, and so on.

★

Efficiency guidelines
1 **Do not waste time reading irrelevant information.**
2 **If notice does not apply, destroy before reading.**
3 **If contents of envelope are inappropriate,
return without opening.**
– The Peter Pyramid *by Laurence J. Peter*

★

Effective Leadership
by John Adair

Check yourself against this ten-point programme once a month for the next six months.

1 *Develop a new personal sense of time*
Do not rely on memory: record where your time goes
2 *Plan ahead*
Make plans on how you are going to spend your time a day, a week, a month, a year ahead. Plan in terms of opportunities and results, priorities and deadlines.
3 *Make the most of your best time*
Programme important tasks for the time of day you function best. Have planned quiet periods for creative thinking.
4 *Capitalise on marginal time*
Squeeze activities into the minutes you spend waiting for a train or between meetings.
5 *Avoid clutter*
Try re-organising your desk for effectiveness. Sort papers into categories according to action priorities. Generate as little paper as possible yourself.
6 *Do it now*
'Procrastination is the thief of time.'
'My object was always to do the business of the day in the day.' (Wellington)

7 *Learn to say No*
Do not let others misappropriate your time.
Decline tactfully but firmly to avoid over-commitment.
8 *Use the telephone as a time-saving tool*
Keep telephone calls down to minimum length.
Screen telephone interruptions.
9 *Delegate*
Learn to delegate as much as possible.
10 *Meetings*
Keep them short.
Sharpen your skills as a chairman.
Cut out unnecessary meetings.

★

What They Don't Teach You at Harvard Business School
by Mark McCormack

Stick to your schedule

Once you have made an itinerary or schedule it is worthless if
you don't stick to it.

A large part of sticking to your schedule is an awareness that
it is very rare that something is so important or a crisis is so
imminent that it has to be attended to immediately. Treat
interruptions or anything else that just comes up as you would
any other time commitment. Don't respond immediately but
programme time for dealing with these situations into your
future schedule – that afternoon, tomorrow or next week –
whenever you have a space to fit them in or can make a space to
fit them in.

The other major aspect of sticking to your schedule is allocating the appropriate amount of time to the activities that will
be filling it up.

It is probably worse to allocate too little time than it is to
allocate too much. This puts you in a position of always having
to catch up, which backs up through your schedule and usually
gets worse as the day wears on.

I think most people can predict with reasonable accuracy how long their usual business activities will take them, but they will often deceive themselves.

To manage time well you have to *believe in your own knowledge*. If you know a weekly meeting takes thirty minutes, don't convince yourself that today it will only take fifteen minutes simply because today you have more to do. If you have to be somewhere in ten minutes and you have ten minutes to get there, don't make one more phone call simply because you want to get it out of the way. People who manage their time badly seem to want to be unrealistic and go out of their way to create out-of-control situations.

★

A desk is a wastebasket with drawers.

STRESS

Time and stress are closely linked for most managers. Horton and Reid highlight some of the ways in which stress can be directed or reduced while McCormack points out that unreasonable expectations lead to unreasonable demands.

Kelso's Observation
**The only one who got everything done by Friday
was Robinson Crusoe.**

★

Enterprise
by Tom Cannon

Stress is a natural part of life. The human body has evolved to cope with anxiety. Some of the physiological responses which occur at the level of the autonomic nervous system improve the body's ability to perform. Adrenaline and noradrenaline are powerful stimulants, speeding up reflexes, increasing heart rate and blood pressure, raising blood sugar levels, and raising bodily metabolism. The result is increased short term capacity and performance, as blood is carried to the muscles and to the lungs, energy supplies are boosted and responses sharpened.

Performance is improved but only for a time and up to a certain level. A reaction is inevitable as the body's ability to cope with this stimulus deteriorates and performance declines. The bell-shaped curve described in research describes the relationship between anxiety and performance.

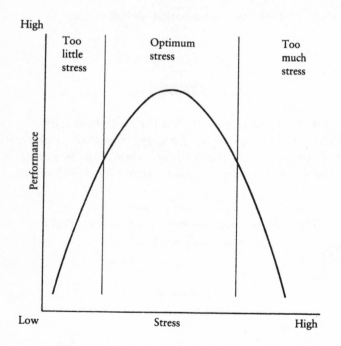

Relationship between anxiety and performance

The adverse effects of a failure to manage stress increase over time. These can include:

- Reduced attention span
- Memory failures
- Aversion to planning
- Irritability
- Sense of powerlessness
- Absenteeism
- Lack of energy
- Unpredictability

- Easily distracted
- Slower responses
- Hypochondria
- Emotionalism
- Speech problem
- Insomnia
- Cynicism

In extreme cases, drug abuse, violence and suicide threats can occur. Action to minimize these risks is the main challenge to stress management.

Recognition of the problem is the precondition for successful action.

★

Beyond the Trust Gap
by Thomas Horton & Peter Reid

Stress busters

- *Try to get away from the job situation during the day, even if only briefly.* Don't pore over reports on your coffee break – do something unrelated to your job.
- *Take vacations – even short ones.* And occasionally, at least once a year, take a real one- or two-week break. For most managers, especially older ones, long weekends just won't do it.
- *Verbalize the problems that are causing stress and anxiety.* Talk to a colleague (whom you can trust to be discreet) or to a friend. Bottled-up anxiety is the worst kind – talking it out can give you a better perspective on the problem.
- *Exercise regularly.* Stress experts say that exercise conditions the body's stress-adaptation mechanisms. But

make sure the exercise is regular, rather than frenzied activity every weekend. How about taking up exercise on your lunch hour?

- *Eat balanced meals as regularly as you can.* Erratic eating habits can aggravate the effects of stress.
- *Get periodic medical checkups.* They occasionally reveal problems of which you might be unaware that may be contributing to symptoms of overreaction to stress.

BUT MOST IMPORTANT:

- Try to negotiate – as an *integral* part of your job – an adequate level of autonomy. Failing this, at least obtain a clear definition of how much control you will have over your work content, your deadlines, and your choice of employees in the unit you manage. Plan and negotiate this at the front end – once you are already in a low-control, high-stress job, it's difficult to bargain your way out of it. Remember: It is not hard work or long hours that create stress, but lack of control.

★

You don't have to be perfect.
– *Mark McCormack*

'I'm warning you, Hotchworth, you're making a career decision here!'

5 High Hopes
Achieving Goals and Motivating Others

Bill Shankly was famous, while he was manager of Liverpool FC, for setting and achieving his goals – in more ways than one. This focus on objectives – setting them, mobilising resources to achieve them and moving on to new targets – is central to the task of management. Despite that, it is surprising how seldom purpose, objective or goal surfaces in the thinking of managers. Job descriptions concentrate on the task to be done. Diaries are crammed with travel, meetings, discussions. Purpose can easily be lost in the routine and even the excitement of doing the job. There is the famous office graffiti about the chief executive about whom it was said, 'What is the difference between X and God?' The reply was, 'God is everywhere, X is everywhere but here.'

This focus on achieving goals is a feature of many of the most successful firms and managers. They get ahead by knowing why they engage in a task and how this task contributes to the overall aims of the firm. Tom Peters highlights the extent to which this approach ensures that existing resources are deployed effectively. New projects, proposals, ideas are accepted or rejected because they contribute, or don't, to the aims of the firm. Sticking to your knitting becomes a meaningful guide rather than merely a catchphrase.

Of course, if people are to contribute to a firm's goals they must know them and understand the ways they can play their part. Mushroom management – keep people in the dark and cover them with manure – remains all too common. Typically, it reflects fear and lack of self-confidence rather than the more common arguments of security or worries about expectations being disappointed. Successful managers tend to assume that colleagues bring their brains to work with them. They can be told when proposals are at an early stage. Changes can be explained far more easily if people know why, rather than being instructed how.

★

I don't want any yes-men around me. I want everybody
to tell me the truth even if it costs them their jobs.
— Samuel Goldwyn

SETTING GOALS

All men seek one goal: success or happiness.
The only way to achieve true success is to express
yourself completely in service to society. First, have a definite,
clear, practical ideal – a goal, an objective. Second, have
the necessary means to achieve your ends –
wisdom, money, materials, and methods.
Third, adjust your means to that end.
— Aristotle

Ambition and determination are part of the attempt to get ahead in business. But you need to know where you are going in order to get there. Schleh's pioneering work on management by objectives highlighted the importance of setting objectives that were reasonable in order to get managers to accept their responsibility. Robert Heller's extensive work on business policy and performance reinforces his belief that goal-setting and achieving results turns on a combination of ownership, involvement and feedback.

Management by Results
by Edward Schleh

Some executives feel that it is good practice to set objectives that are far out in 'the wild blue yonder.' In other words, they feel that it is sound to set objectives that are almost impossible to attain. 'Give them something to shoot for.' This philosophy is ordinarily based on an unrealistic approach to human beings and their motivation. *Objectives should be reasonable.* It takes a great deal of fortitude and drive for a man to consistently react well to an objective set beyond his reach. In most cases such an objective will take the heart out of a good man rather than be a stimulus to him to work harder. People are usually more stimulated by success than they are by failure. In addition, if goals are too stiff, a man may begin to accept non-accomplishment as normal and lose his sense of personal accountability – the real driving force that spurs men on in any operation.

★

The Decision Makers
by Robert Heller

Positive rules for decision-makers who want to achieve excellent results:

1 Involve all relevant people from the start.
2 Have a single, fully worked out object in view – aim to kill one bird with many stones, not two birds with one.
3 Having obtained the best possible information and counsel in concert, act on it in concert.
4 Be governed by what you know, rather than what you fear.
5 Embody the decisions in a comprehensive plan that everybody knows and that will cover the expected consequences of setback or success.
6 Entrust its execution to competent people with no conflicting responsibilities.
7 Leave operational people to operate.
8 In the event of serious failure, start again to review and renew the decisions.
9 Only abandon the decision when it is plain to all that its objectives cannot be achieved.

ACCOUNTABILITY

Human beings were held accountable long before there
were corporate bureaucracies. If the knight didn't
deliver, the king cut off his head.
— Across the Board *by Alvin Toffler*

*Goals once set must be achieved. It is this personal responsibility
for achievement that set the manager apart from the administrator.*

Management by Results
by Edward Schleh

Accountability must be personal

Basically, accountability means this: *If an objective is delegated
to a man, he must feel a sense of obligation for its accomplishment.* If it is accomplished, he, personally, will be given full
credit for it. If it is not, he knows that he will get the discredit.
Note the implication of the word 'feel'. Accountability is
meaningless until it gets down to the personal feelings of the
individual. The man must feel that it applies to him and no one
else. This is forgotten by many executives in their wish to adhere
to a democratic principle. Committee meetings, coordinators,
and communications are usually poor substitutes.

TEAMS

*Perhaps the hardest part of the link between setting and achieving goals lies in winning the involvement and commitment of
others. Teams succeed by sharing these goals, compensating
for each other's weaknesses and making sure that together they
produce more than the sum of their parts. Tom Peters
highlights the ways in which this 'added value' distinguishes
teams from committees and other bureaucratic structures
which often emerge in large organizations to protect staff from
their customers and the 'real work' identified by Schumacher.*

Liberation Management
by Tom Peters

Don't let project teams become committees

Project structures aren't new. 'Task forces' were the rage for a while. The matrix structure was an effort to create more fluid, responsive enterprises – but committee-itis and a lack of accountability caused it to misfire. The project structure's key success variables turn out to be *outward focus*, *autonomy/accountability*, and *dependence*. The McKinsey project team, with just three people, is *focused on the customer*; it's *unmistakably accountable*; and, thanks to the nature and intensity of the work, *each team member depends upon the others* for personal and company success. That's no committee!

Here are a baker's dozen of must-do's to keep you on the straight and narrow:

- Set goals/deadlines for key subsystem tests.
- Keep team members' destiny in the hands of the project leader.
- Aim for full-time assignment to the team.
- Give members authority to commit their functions.
- Allot space so that team members can 'live' together.
- Remember the social element.
- Allow outsiders in.
- Construct self-contained systems.
- Let teams pick their own leaders.
- Let teams spend/approve their own travel, etc.
- Honour project leadership skills.
- Honour project membership skills.

★

Small Is Beautiful
by E. F. Schumacher

Think of the therapeutic value of real work; think of its educational value. No one would then want to raise the school-leaving age or to lower the retirement age, so as to keep people off the labour market. Everybody would be welcome to lend a hand. Everybody would be admitted to what is now the rarest privilege, the opportunity of working usefully, creatively, with his own hands and brains, in his own time, at his own pace – and with excellent tools. Would this mean an enormous extension of working hours? No, people who work in this way do not know the difference between work and leisure. Unless they sleep or eat or occasionally choose to do nothing at all, they are always agreeably, productively engaged. Many of the 'on-cost jobs' would simply disappear; I leave it to the reader's imagination to identify them. There would be little need for mindless entertainment or other drugs, and unquestionably much less illness.

MOTIVATION

Wain's Fifth Conclusion
**Nothing motivates a man more than to see
his boss putting in an honest day's work.**

Schumacher's advocacy of an economics in which 'people matter' increases in relevance as the human edge is increasing the business edge. Getting the best out of people is seen by companies like Teleflex as the most effective way to get the best out of their firm. The burgeoning recognition that a highly motivated and committed workforce can provide the difference between success and failure is forcing managers to look for ways to help people reach their full potential.

Sometimes, this means nothing more than recognizing their

contribution, making them feel important or converting negative feelings of powerlessness into positive feelings of value. Firms like Virgin have designed their entire operation to encourage personal enterprise or intrapreneurship.

Thriving on Chaos
by Tom Peters

Bim Black revitalized Teleflex, a $150 million applications engineering company (sophisticated valves, control systems, coatings), by installing a vigorous, decentralized entrepreneurial style in a formerly hidebound organization. A strong people philosophy was at the heart of it:

- People are people . . . not personnel.
- People don't dislike work . . . help them to understand mutual objectives and they'll drive themselves to unbelievable excellence.
- The best way to really train people is with an experienced mentor . . . and on the job.
- People have ego and development needs . . . and they'll commit themselves only to the extent that they can see ways of satisfying these needs.
- People cannot be truly motivated by anyone else . . . that door is locked from the inside; they should work in an atmosphere that fosters self-motivation . . . self-assessment . . . and self-confidence.
- People should work in a climate that is challenging, invigorating, and fun . . . and the rewards should be related as directly as possible to performance.
- When people are in an atmosphere of trust, they'll put themselves at risk; only through risk is there growth . . . reward . . . self-confidence . . . leadership.

★

> **Help people reach their full potential.**
> **Catch them doing something right.**
> – The One Minute Manager
> *by Kenneth Blanchard & Spencer Johnson*

★

What They Don't Teach You at Harvard Business School
by Mark McCormack

Basically, people aren't inconsistent, but their behaviour is. . .
I have four general philosophies for dealing with employees:

1 Pay them what they are worth
2 Make them feel that they are important, yet
3 Make them think for themselves, and
4 Separate office life from social life.

★

Zapp!
by William C. Byham & Jeff Cox

When you have been *Sapped*, you feel like . . .

- Your job belongs to the company.
- You are just doing whatever you are told.
- Your job doesn't really matter.
- You don't know how well you're doing.
- You always have to keep your mouth shut.
- Your job is something different from who you are.
- You have little or no control over your work.

When you have been *Zapped*, you feel like . . .

- Your job belongs to you.
- You are responsible.
- Your job counts for something.
- You know where you stand.

- You have some say in how things are done.
- Your job is a part of who you are.
- You have some control over your work.

★

**'Involvement' in this context differs from 'commitment'
in the same sense as the pig's and the chicken's roles
in one's breakfast of ham and eggs. The chicken was involved –
the pig was committed.**

★

From a paper on 'Entrepreneurship'
by Richard Branson

My philosophy of motivation can be summed up under the heading 'Small is Beautiful'.

In the early days, we could certainly not have afforded a lavish corporate headquarters in central London. But now we don't have one as a matter of choice. It's not just that people seem to prefer working in smaller units, but it helps to avoid some of the hazards of growth, and especially the tendency for managers to lose touch with the basics – and usually the customers and the staff.

So when one of our companies gets beyond a certain size, we split it up into smaller units. Even though Virgin Records was, before we sold it to Thorn EMI, the sixth largest record company in the world, we managed through a series of semi-independent labels and subsidiaries in twenty countries.

This 'keep it small' rule gives us the opportunity to pursue a policy of promoting from within the Group – a policy which clearly has a positive effect on morale. It means you can give more than the usual number of managers the challenge and excitement of running their own business. The kind of people I want running Virgin companies are those who would probably become millionaires if they weren't working for us. So if you can give them a stake in the company, they can become millionaires by working within Virgin.

And this, by the way, is I believe the only way to encourage entrepreneurship from within the company – or Intrapreneurship, as I believe the academics call it.

DEMOTIVATION

Richard Branson's approach contrasts sharply with the self-centred approach of the old-style 'moguls' described by Heller. They gained much of their personal satisfaction from the power they exercised. The demotivating effect this had on their staff was irrelevant even if it undermined performance. Problems of demotivation face leaders and managers in all walks of life. Montgomery recognized that unless his demotivated troops were re-motivated they could never defeat Rommel's forces. His crushing victories in the desert were founded on the belief among the troops that they could and would win.

The Decision Makers
by Robert Heller

The moguls always involve all relevant people, because only one person qualifies: themselves. They characteristically concentrate on single, great objectives; they are fearless; they know exactly what they are doing and why; they automatically adapt and adjust to failure; they only persist with it up to the point of no return; if they still see the prospect of a ripe pay-off, they stick octopus-like to their task.

In all this, because they follow no consensus save that inside their own heads, their actions, despite frequent appearances to the contrary, are generally coherent and clearly motivated. The one point . . . which they consistently ignore is leaving operating people to operate. These decision-makers interfere constantly, in fair weather and foul. Their whole method presupposes underlings who will do only one thing – what they are told. At this point, tycoonery and judge and jury come together. Like the legal judge, the tycoon depends on the warders and hangman to obey his orders in utterly predictable conformity. So he needs predictable conformists, without imagination, independence or pride.

★

'Just for the minutes, did anyone manage to catch the chairman's parting words?'

★

Powerlessness corrupts.
Absolute powerlessness corrupts absolutely.
– Rosabeth Moss Kanter

★

If you've got them by the balls,
their hearts and minds will soon follow.
– Charles Colson, special assistant
to President Richard M. Nixon

★

– Field Marshal Lord Montgomery on arrival at the 8th Army,
quoted in Effective Leadership *by John Adair*

'I understand there has been a great deal of "belly-aching" out here. By "belly-aching" I mean inventing poor reasons for not doing what one has been told to do.

'All this is to stop at once.

'I will tolerate no belly-aching. If anyone objects to doing what he is told, then he can get out of it; and at once. I want that made very clear right down through the Eighth Army.

'I have little more to say just at present. And some of you may think it is quite enough and may wonder if I am mad. I assure you I am quite sane.

'I understand there are people who often think I am slightly mad; so often that I now regard it as rather a compliment.

'All I have to say to that is that if I am slightly mad, there are a large number of people I could name who are raving lunatics.

'What I have done is to get over to you the 'atmosphere' in which we will now work and fight; you must see that that atmosphere permeates right down through the Eighth Army to the most junior private soldier. All the soldiers must know what is wanted; when they see it coming to pass there will be a surge of confidence throughout the army.

'I ask you to give me your confidence and to have faith that what I have said will come to pass.

'There is much work to be done. The orders I have given about no further withdrawal will mean a complete change in the layout of our dispositions; also that we must begin to prepare for our great offensive.

'The great point to remember is that we are going to finish with this chap Rommel once and for all. It will be quite easy. There is no doubt about it.

'He is definitely a nuisance. Therefore we will hit him a crack and finish with him.'

No systems of organization are more closely linked with de-motivation and low morale than bureaucracies. Ogden's Observation that 'it is the pleasure bureaucracies get out of causing difficulties that makes them so powerful' highlights the way the problems of a bureaucracy extend far beyond its confines. Parkinson highlights not only the stultifying nature of bureaucracies but the problems of rooting out their influences.

Parkinson's Law
by C. Northcote Parkinson

Injelititis or Palsied Paralysis

We find everywhere a type of organization (administrative, commercial, or academic) in which the higher officials are plodding and dull, those less senior are active only in intrigue against each other, and the junior men are frustrated or frivolous. Little is being attempted. Nothing is being achieved. And in contemplating this sorry picture, we conclude that those in control have done their best, struggled against adversity, and have finally admitted defeat. It now appears from the results of recent investigation, that no such failure need be assumed. In a high percentage of the moribund institutions so far examined the final state of coma is something gained of set purpose and after prolonged effort. It is the result, admittedly, of a disease, but of a disease that is largely self-induced. From the first signs of the condition, the progress of the disease has been encouraged, the causes aggravated, and the symptoms welcomed. It is the disease of induced inferiority, called Injelititis. It is a commoner ailment than is often supposed, and the diagnosis is far easier than the cure.

NO-NO's

In part, these problems occur because the bureaucracies and their corrupting effect grew slowly. Just as the road to hell is paved with good intentions, the route to bureaucracy is built on minor privileges. Reserved parking spaces seem like a good idea when suggested at the board meeting. They avoid unpleasant scenes and unnecessary delays. But, like the rest of the paraphernalia identified by Townsend overleaf, they merely serve to insulate managers from reality.

Further Up the Organisation
by Robert Townsend

- *Reserved parking spaces.* If you're so bloody important, you better be first one in the office. Besides, you'll meet a nice class of people in the employees' parking lot.
- *Special-quality stationery* for the boss and his elite.
- *Muzak,* except in the areas where the work is only suitable for mental defectives.
- *Bells and buzzers* (even telephones can be made to signal with lights).
- *Company shrinks.* Unless it's really optional, and the shrink reports only to the patient, and suitable precautions have been taken to make sure the personnel department can't tap into the data.
- *Outside directorships and trusteeships* for the chief executive. Give up all those non-jobs. You can't even run your own company, dummy.
- *Company plane.* It's just a variation of the company-paid golf club, and the big office with three secretaries. Another line drawn through the company between the Brahmins and the untouchables. And the plane's always in Palm Beach, Augusta, Aspen, or Las Vegas when the business needs it.
- *Manager's Monthly.* Or any other time-consuming report imposed on the troops by 'top' management. It's a joke because it consumes ten pounds of energy to produce each ounce of misunderstanding.
- *Except* in poker, bridge, and similar play-period activities, don't con anybody.

Not your wife	Not your suppliers
Not your children	Not your regulatory authorities
Not your employees	Not even your competitors
Not your customers	
Not your stockholders	
Not your boss	
Not your associates	

'Sorry. We only whistle while we work.'

6 Imagine
Strategies and Scenarios

In Alice Through the Looking Glass, *Alice has a conversation with the Cheshire Cat on the following lines:*

> 'Would you tell me, please, which way
> I ought to go from here?'
> 'That depends a good deal on where
> you want to get to,' said the Cat.
> 'I don't much care where,' said Alice,
> 'so long as I get somewhere.'
> 'Then it doesn't matter which way
> you go,' said the Cat.

There are many managers today who could easily identify with this situation. Nothing is more closely identified with failure in business than the lack of a sense of direction. It puts the firm on the defensive against its rivals, fighting on territory of their choosing rather than grounds which serve its interest best. Understanding strategy and its role in business development is an integral part of success.

Michael Porter's work has had a profound effect on current thinking about getting ahead in business by winning a competitive advantage. His work links some well-established truths about the value of scenario analysis linked with an ability to adapt flexibly to changing circumstances, with a powerful analysis of the ways in which competitive advantage can be won and sustained. Much of the current interest in strategy in Europe and North America was prompted by the evidence which has emerged on the attention paid in Japanese companies to linking a powerful sense of direction with a determined effort to mobilize corporate resources to achieve these goals. The strength of approach turns on the successful integration of the two halves of this proposition. These are, *first, knowing where you are going and, second, making sure that everyone is fully committed to implementing these goals. This latter has led to a restatement of the old FIFO maxim. It used to mean 'First, In, First Out'. Now, it means 'Fit In, (or) F*** Off'.*

★

Weakness comes from having to prepare against possible attacks . . . strength, from compelling our adversary to make these preparations against us.
— Sun Tzu

THE NATURE OF STRATEGY

One of the most positive features of recent management writing is the emphasis placed on strategy and direction. If firms know where they are going, they are more likely to get there. Understanding the nature of strategy and the distinction between strategic, tactical and other decisions is the first step in establishing a sense of direction and vision in a firm.

★

The Characteristics of Strategic Decisions
Important
Long time horizon
Involve top decision makers
Match activities to resources
Demand major resources
Deal with unstructured and unique problems
Shape the firm's activities
Involve subjective judgement
Are complex
Make evaluation difficult
— Basic Marketing *by Tom Cannon*

★

> The aim of strategy is to reach a decisive battle
> by creating and using a situation which
> undermines the enemy's morale sufficiently to
> enable him to accept the conditions one wishes
> to impose upon him.
> — *Beaufre*

ANALYSIS

Dr Boyson's Rule
When policy fails, try thinking.

Interest in strategy and direction owes much to the emphasis placed by Japanese firms on strategic thinking. The most successful of these firms are characterized by a willingness to invest time in understanding the contexts in which their strategies will operate. Few people have managed to penetrate this way of thinking more successfully than Ken Ohmae of McKinsey in Japan. The proper appreciation of a firm's Strengths, Weaknesses, Opportunities and Threats of the type described by Scott is the foundation stone for this type of review of capabilities. Awareness of the firm's own situation gains extra value if the strategists can get inside the thinking of rivals in the way described in the extract from Barbarians at the Gate.

The Mind of the Strategist
by Kenichi Ohmae

Analysis is the critical starting point of strategic thinking. Faced with problems, trends, events, or situations that appear to constitute a harmonious whole or come packaged as a whole by the common sense of the day, the strategic thinker dissects them into their constituent parts. Then, having discovered the significance of these constituents, he reassembles them in a way calculated to maximize his advantage.

In business as on the battlefield, the object of strategy is to bring about the conditions most favourable to one's own side, judging precisely the right moment to attack or withdraw and always assessing the limits of compromise correctly. Besides the habit of analysis, what marks the mind of the strategist is an intellectual elasticity or flexibility that enables him to come up with realistic responses to changing situations, not simply to discriminate with great precision among different shades of grey.

★

Into Profit
by Bill Scott

- *Strengths*
  Be careful that you do not take too rosy a view of your strengths. What is important are *comparative* strengths, the areas where you are relatively stronger than the competition. For example, the fact that you have the very latest high-technology production process may only really be a strength if the competitors do not also have it. If they do not, then the possibility of their acquiring it may be a threat.
- *Weaknesses*
  A weakness is a weakness, even if all the competition share that same weakness. The fact that they have the same weakness as you may be an opportunity, provided you correct your own weakness first.
- *Opportunities*
  Many of the opportunities will fall out of your analysis of how attractive the market is, especially where there is growth or a gap in the market. Others may exist due to some weakness in the competitors' armour. The possibility of innovation on your part may be one of your biggest opportunities.
- *Threats or risks*
  We have already noted many possible risks as we analysed the market and the industry structure. Your exposure to

product substitution, to cyclical patterns, to possible new competitors and the risk attaching to your customer profile or your supplier profile could all very well be threats. So too could a major innovation by a competitor.

In doing a SWOT analysis you have to keep things in some perspective. The first time round you may very well fill several pages. Now go back and 'sore-thumb' it:

* Concentrate on what really is important.
* If an item is trivial, delete it.
* Unless you can establish cause and effect, cross that item off the list.

The next step in the thinking will be far too complex if you have anything other than the really important items to take into account.

★

Barbarians at the Gate
by Bryan Burrough & John Helyar

Cliff Robbins had laid out their options in a memo for the 'Project Peach' team that day.

There were three. First was a so-called bear hug letter to the board. In it, Kravis would signal his interest to pay more than $75 a share but stop short of an outright offer. Under the 'Advantages' column, Robbins noted, a bear hug would probably get them access to confidential RJR Nabisco financial information, a must if they weren't bidding with a management team. It would also stall the management group's drive to quickly sew up the deal. Under 'Disadvantages,' Robbins worried that a threatening letter would only lead to an extended auction. Bidding, the memo noted, 'would go to the edge of the envelope.' They might win, he concluded, but it could cost them billions in the process.

The second option was a meeting with Shearson and

Johnson, perhaps to discuss a joint bid. 'Shows weakness?' the memo asked. Third was a tender offer, the blitzkrieg approach counselled by Wasserstein. The upside: 'Seizes timing advantage . . . stalls management deal.' The downside: 'No information . . . hostile . . . financing hurdles.'

When it came time for the advisers to speak, Eric Cleacher went first. His speech was almost military in tone, the kind of talk one delivers to a boot camp or at halftime of a crucial football game. Gleacher, a jock and proud of it, had the macho intensity characteristic of some small men.

'You've got to do a tender offer,' Gleacher said. 'The risk here is that Shearson'll have some kind of contract with the board before we can do something. If you call 'em back and say, "Yeah, we're interested," we end up getting pushed around. A tender offer puts us on even footing. We have to be firm here. It's very important from a symbolic point. . . . We've got to move fast. We've got to follow 'em out of the water. Just blow 'em right away.'

Across the table Dick Beattie grinned. It was vintage Gleacher.

Wasserstein went next, essentially repeating the message he had given Kravis privately the night before. The discussion continued, with the pros and cons of each move pored over in detail. Drexel's Leon Black sounded a cautionary note. 'Gee, what's the hurry? Why don't we just wait and top it?'

'Then you're the bad guys,' Gleacher said.

They talked further, but it was clear which way the group was leaning.

'What price?' Kravis asked.

'Maybe we should do it at seventy-five,' Gleacher suggested.

Wasserstein shook his head. 'Somewhere in the nineties, I think.' Competitors joked that Wasserstein's pocketbook was always open, at least when it was a client's money he was spending. His clients regularly bid so high traders spoke of a 'Wasserstein Premium.'

Kravis turned to Steve Waters, who knew Johnson better than anyone at the table.

'How do you read Johnson?' Kravis asked.

Waters rattled through Johnson's track record, concluding, 'Ross never bought anything. He's always been a seller.' A $90 tender offer would immediately put him on the defensive. For one thing, he wouldn't want to match it. But more important, compared to the $75 proposal already on the table, a $90 bid would make it appear Johnson was stealing the company. If so, they could hope to drive a crucial wedge between Johnson and his board.

'If we come on strong,' Waters added, 'he might fold.' . . .

After hurriedly finishing dinner, the five general partners piled into Kravis's blue Mercedes 500. They were at Skadden within minutes. Upstairs, Kravis, Roberts, and Raether were escorted into a conference room, where they were met by Felix Rohatyn, Ira Harris, and Peter Atkins.

Kravis looked for signs of the management group, but saw none. Rohatyn began reeling through a list of open issues. Lazard and Dillon, he said, wanted to learn more about the securities Kravis proposed to include in his offer. There were some other points, all minor. Then Rohatyn asked, 'Is this your best offer?'

'Yes,' Kravis said.

'Well, if we can work out the securities and get comfortable with regard to the financing, we are prepared to recommend your bid to the special committee.'

Kravis and Roberts broke into smiles.

A winner.

SCENARIOS AND RESPONSES

Scenario analysis enables managers and firms to test their analysis and the resulting strategies against different situations. Michael Porter of Harvard Business School extended this notion to integrate the options open to firms' particular assets and characteristics. These are mobilised to win competitive advantage. His analysis showed that firms had a bundle of attributes which were powerful competitive tools under different market conditions. Understanding these conditions or scenarios and developing responses based on specific company attributes is an important first step in gaining advantage over rivals.

Competitive Advantage
by Michael Porter

Strategic approaches under scenarios

1 *Bet on the most probable scenario*
In this approach, the firm designs its strategy around the scenario (or range of scenarios) that is seen to be most probable, accepting the risk that it may not occur. . . .

In practice, betting on the most probable scenario is a common approach to strategy formulation under uncertainty though it is done implicitly. Managers often base their strategies on implicit assumptions about the future. Without becoming explicit, however, a scenario may be based on ignorance and may fail the test of internal consistency so critical to good planning under uncertainty.

2 *Bet on the 'best' scenario*
In this approach, a firm designs its strategies for the scenario in which the firm can establish the most sustainable long-run competitive advantage given its initial position and resources. This approach seeks the highest upside potential by tuning the strategy to the possible future industry structure that yields the best outcome for the firm. The risk, of course, is that the best scenario does not occur and the chosen strategy is thereby inappropriate.

3 *Hedge*
In this approach, a firm chooses a strategy that produces satisfactory results under all scenarios, or at least under all scenarios that are deemed to have an appreciable probability of occurring. This is one approach to designing a robust

strategy. The idea is similar to the 'minimax' strategy in game theory, where a player makes the move that minimizes his maximum loss. Hedging might entail developing a very wide model line, or entering nondealer channels with slightly different models sold under a different brand name at the same time as the firm continued to serve dealers.

4 *Preserve flexibility*
Another approach to dealing with uncertain scenarios is to choose a strategy that preserves flexibility until it becomes more apparent which scenario will actually occur. This is another way of creating a robust strategy and illustrates that robustness must be carefully defined. The firm postpones resource commitments that lock it into a particular strategy. Once the uncertainties begin to resolve themselves, a strategy that fits the scenario that appears to be occurring is chosen, taking into account the firm's resources and skills. . . .

5 *Influence*
In the final approach to addressing uncertainty, a firm attempts to use its resources to bring about a scenario that it considers desirable. A firm seeks to raise the odds that a scenario will occur for which it has a competitive advantage. Doing so requires that a firm try to influence the causal factors behind the scenario variables. Since a causal factor in casual user demand for chain saws is woodburning stove installations, for example, a firm might try to influence stove demand. This might involve coalitions with woodburning stove manufacturers, or advertising that stressed the value of woodburning stoves at the same time that it advertised chain saws. Technological changes, channel policies, government regulation, and many other sources of uncertainty can sometimes be influenced. The possibility for influence and its cost must be weighed against the competitive advantage to be gained if a firm can raise the odds that its preferred scenario will occur.

Inherent in Porter's approach is the belief that firms and their managers can make choices about the ways to deploy their resources and skills. Ohmae's strategists are not mechanics who get ahead by mechanically designing strategies from fixed ingredients, but 'artists' creating new realities from current ingredients.

The Mind of the Strategist
by Kenichi Ohmae

Successful business strategies result not from rigorous analysis but from a particular state of mind. In what I call the mind of the strategist, insight and a consequent drive for achievement, often amounting to a sense of mission, fuel a thought process which is basically creative and intuitive rather than rational. Strategists do not reject analysis. Indeed they can hardly do without it. But they use it only to stimulate the creative process, to test the ideas that emerge, to work out their strategic implications, or to ensure successful execution of high-potential 'wild' ideas that might otherwise never be implemented properly. Great strategies, like great works of art or great scientific discoveries, call for technical mastery in the working out but originate in insights that are beyond the reach of conscious analysis.

COMPETITIVENESS

Managers do not have a free hand in deploying resources and executing strategies. Prahalad and Hamel show how it is the ability of firms to consolidate their strengths into 'core competencies' that provides a competitive edge over rivals. These competencies are 'the glue that binds existing businesses'. They define the areas in which the firm can succeed and those in which the risk of failure is highest.

'The Core Competence of the Corporation'
by C. K. Prahalad & G. Hamel

The roots of competitive advantage

In the short run, a company's competitiveness derives from the price/performance attributes of current products. But the survivors of the first wave of global competition, Western and Japanese alike, are all converging on similar and formidable standards for product cost and quality – minimum hurdles for continued competition, but less and less important as sources of differential advantage. In the long run, competitiveness derives from an ability to build, at lower cost and more speedily than competitors, the core competencies that spawn unanticipated products. The real sources of advantage are to be found in management's ability to consolidate corporate-wide technologies and production skills into competencies that empower individual businesses to adapt quickly to changing opportunities.

Senior executives who claim that they cannot build core competencies either because they feel the autonomy of business units is sacrosanct or because their feet are held to the quarterly budget fire should think again. The problem in many Western companies is not that their senior executives are any less capable than those in Japan nor that Japanese companies possess greater technical capabilities. Instead, it is their adherence to a concept of the corporation that unnecessarily limits the ability of individual businesses to fully exploit the deep reservoir of technological capability that many American and European companies possess. . . .

Core competencies are the collective learning in the organization, especially how to coordinate diverse production skills and integrate multiple streams of technologies. Consider Sony's capacity to miniaturize or Philips's optical-media expertise. The theoretical knowledge to put a radio on a chip does not in itself assure a company the skill to produce a miniature radio no bigger than a business card. To bring off this feat,

Casio must harmonize know-how in miniaturization, microprocessor design, material science, and ultra-thin precision casing – the same skills it applies in its miniature card calculators, pocket TVs, and digital watches.

If core competence is about harmonizing streams of technology, it is also about the organization of work and the delivery of value. Among Sony's competencies is miniaturization. To bring miniaturization to its products, Sony must ensure that technologists, engineers, and marketers have a shared understanding of customer needs and of technological possibilities. The force of core competence is felt as decisively in services as in manufacturing. Citicorp was ahead of others investing in an operating system that allowed it to participate in world markets 24 hours a day. Its competence in systems has provided the company the means to differentiate itself from many financial service institutions.

Core competence is communication, involvement, and a deep commitment to working across organizational boundaries. It involves many levels of people and all functions. World-class research in, for example, lasers or ceramics can take place in corporate laboratories without having an impact on any of the businesses of the company. The skills that together constitute core competence must coalesce around individuals whose efforts are not so narrowly focused that they cannot recognize the opportunities for blending their functional expertise with those of others in new and interesting ways.

Core competence does not diminish with use. Unlike physical assets, which do deteriorate over time, competencies are enhanced as they are applied and shared. But competencies still need to be nurtured and protected, knowledge fades if it is not used. Competencies are the glue that binds existing businesses. They are also the engine for new business development. Patterns of diversification and market entry may be guided by them, not just by the attractiveness of markets. . . .

In contrast, there are major companies that have had the potential to build core competencies but failed to do so because top management was unable to conceive of the company as anything other than a collection of discrete businesses.

★

The expert commander strikes only when the situation assures victory. To create such a situation is the ultimate responsibility of generalship. Before he gives battle the superior general causes the enemy to disperse. When the enemy disperses and attempts to defend everywhere he is weak everywhere, and at the selected points many will be able to strike his few.

– Sun Tzu

★

Competitive Strategy
by Michael Porter

Dimensions of competitive strategy

Companies' strategies for competing in an industry can differ in a wide variety of ways. However, the following strategic dimensions usually capture the possible differences among a company's strategic options in a given industry.

- *Specialization*: the degree to which it focuses its efforts in terms of the width of its line, the target customer segments, and the geographic markets served.
- *Brand identification*: the degree to which it seeks brand identification rather than competition based mainly on price or other variables. Brand identification can be achieved via advertising, sales force, or a variety of other means.
- *Push versus pull*: the degree to which it seeks to develop brand identification with the ultimate consumer directly versus the support of distribution channels in selling its product.

- *Channel selections*: the choice of distribution channels ranging from company-owned channels to specialty outlets to broadline outlets.
- *Product quality*: its level of product quality, in terms of raw materials, specifications, adherence to tolerances, features, and so on.
- *Technological leadership*: the degree to which it seeks technological leadership versus following or imitation. It is important to note that a firm could be a technological leader but deliberately not produce the highest quality product in the market; quality and technological leadership do not necessarily go together.
- *Vertical integration*: the extent of value added as reflected in the level of forward and backward integration adopted, including whether the firm has captive distribution, exclusive or owned retail outlets, an in-house service network, and so on.
- *Cost position*: the extent to which it seeks the low-cost position in manufacturing and distribution through investment in cost-minimizing facilities and equipment.
- *Service*: the degree to which it provides ancillary services with its product line, such as engineering assistance, an in-house service network, credit, and so forth. This aspect of strategy could be viewed as part of vertical integration but is usefully separated for analytical purposes.
- *Price policy*: its relative price position in the market. Price position will usually be related to such other variables as cost position and product quality, but price is a distinct strategic variable that must be treated separately.
- *Leverage*: the amount of financial leverage and operating leverage it bears.
- *Relationship with parent company*: requirements on the behaviour of the unit based on the relationship between a unit and its parent company. The firm could be a unit of a highly diversified conglomerate, one of a vertical chain of businesses, part of a cluster of related businesses in a general sector, a subsidiary of a foreign company, and so

on. The nature of the relationship with the parent will influence the objectives with which the firm is managed, the resources available to it, and perhaps determine some operations or functions that it shares with other units (with resulting cost implications).

• *Relationship to home and host government*: in international industries, the relationship the firm has developed or is subject to with its home government as well as host governments in foreign countries where it is operating. Home governments can provide resources or other assistance to the firm, or conversely can regulate the firm or otherwise influence its goals. Host governments often play similar roles.

Each of these strategic dimensions can be described for a firm at differing levels of detail, and other dimensions might be added to refine the analysis; the important thing is that these dimensions provide an overall picture of the firm's position.

VISIONS AND GOALS

It is, however, the way the competencies described earlier by Prahalad and Hamel are directed to achieve specific goals or visions that determines the long-term nature and shape of the firm. John Sculley uses his experiences, in top management at Pepsi and Apple to balance the relative merits of visions and goals as the starting point for strategic planning. He opts for the flexibility provided by goals. Pascale uses the results of his research at Stanford University to introduce a different perspective. This emphasizes the value that can come from flexibility in strategic perspective. Sometimes it is right to emphasize the controls imposed by plans, while on other occasions opportunism is the key to success.

Odyssey: From Pepsi to Apple
by John Sculley

I like directions better than goals. While the genetic code is predetermined, it's not fixed as habit/culture is. In America, projects have a beginning, a middle, and an end. In Japan, projects have direction, so that what you're pushing for is heading further and further out.

We don't try so much to define Apple's identity; instead, we try to make it recognizable.

★

Managing on the Edge
by Richard Pascale

Strategy: planned versus opportunistic

Most Fortune 500 companies engage in some type of strategic planning. Business schools devote many semester credits to strategic analysis, and consultants develop elaborate matrices to advance thinking in this realm. There are, of course, instances in which strategic analysis played an important role in shaping a corporation's actions, but more often than not, strategic planning and formal analysis play a secondary role in explaining the home runs that occur now and then. Many business breakthroughs result from an opportunistic response: someone has a new idea, it matches a market niche, and soon a new business is budding. Only after the fact are premeditated designs attributed to these outcomes. Conversely, companies that are opportunistic to the extreme often wind up like Atari: managerial umbrellas for a loose band of entrepreneurs. There was a lot of energy and initiative, but the organization as a whole didn't cleave together.

Neither 'planned' nor 'opportunistic' *extremes* alone provide the long-term answer. Organizations need both. The answer lies in a 'dynamic synthesis' – not a compromise or mathematical halfway house of strategic and opportunistic tendencies, but a *paradoxical embrace* that contains both poles.

★

enterprise (n.) making toeless shoes a fashion
instead of a calamity.
— The Wit's Dictionary, *ed. Colin Bowles*

John Harvey-Jones draws out the oversimplification that often occurs in discussion of business strategy. This is the over-emphasis given to victory and defeat. In practice, business rivalry is more like the middle game of a chess match than the end game. The emphasis is on the struggle for position, not the knock-out blow. This is a view endorsed by Pirsig, who empha-sizes the importance of deep reflection over hurried thought. The kind of systematic analysis employed by Porter needs proper reflection based on the type of coherent structure he proposes.

Making It Happen
by John Harvey-Jones

Establishing with clarity the starting point of a business is rather like playing three-dimensional chess. You have first of all to decide where you are, or where the business stands relative to where it has come from because that indeed will produce the current direction and speed of movement . . . If establishing where you are relative to your own past and producing your future trajectory is difficult, assessing your position in relation to your competitors' strengths, weaknesses, position and strategies is even more so.

★

Zen and the Art of Motor Cycle Maintenance
by Robert Pirsig

He was thinking too hard, and the harder you think in this high country of the mind the slower you go . . . It's frustrating to see how completely unaware he is at the time of the significance of what he is saying. It's like seeing someone handling, one by one, all the pieces of a jigsaw puzzle whose solution you know, and you want to tell him, 'Look, this fits here, and this fits here,' but you can't tell him. And so he wanders blindly along one trial after another gathering one piece after another and wondering what to do with them and you grit your teeth when he goes off on a false trail and you are relieved when he comes back again, even though he is discouraged himself. 'Don't worry,' you want to tell him. 'Keep going.'

★

Competitive Strategy
by Michael Porter

Generic strategies

Implementing the generic strategies successfully requires different resources and skills. The generic strategies also imply differing organizational arrangements, control procedures, and inventive systems. As a result, sustained commitment to one of the strategies as the primary target is usually necessary to achieve success. Some common implications of the generic strategies in these areas are as follows:

Generic Strategy	Commonly Required Skills and Resources	Common Organizational Requirements
Overall Cost Leadership	• Sustained capital investment and access to capital • Process engineering skills • Intense supervision of labour • Products designed for ease in manufacture • Low-cost distribution system	• Tight cost control • Frequent, detailed control reports • Structured organization and responsibilities • Incentives based on meeting strict quantitative targets

Generic Strategy	Commonly Required Skills and Resources	Common Organizational Requirements
Differentiation	• Strong marketing abilities • Product engineering • Creative flair • Strong capability in basic research • Corporate reputation for quality or technological leadership • Long tradition in the industry or unique combination of skills drawn from other businesses • Strong cooperation from channels	• Strong coordination among functions in R&D, product development, and marketing • Subjective measurement and incentives instead of quantitative measures • Amenities to attract highly skilled labour, scientists, or creative people
Focus	• Combination of the above policies directed at the particular strategic target	• Combination of the above policies directed at the particular strategic target

The generic strategies may also require different styles of leadership and can translate into very different corporate cultures and atmospheres. Different sorts of people will be attracted.

★

In battle, there are not more than two methods
of attack – the direct and the indirect. In all
fighting, the direct method may be used for joining
battle, but indirect methods will be needed in
order to secure victory.
– *Sun Tzu*

★

'Is this a serious take-over bid, Carruthers?'

PORTFOLIOS

*The shift in attitudes towards inter-firm rivalry explicitly
acknowledges the diversified nature of many firms, especially
large companies. They offer a range of products and services.
These constitute their portfolio. Some will be in the ascendant,*

others will be in decline, while elsewhere it is impossible to draw a firm conclusion. Getting the best from the portfolio is far more important than exploiting a specific opportunity or offering. Michael Porter links the strategies available to the firm to the different ways in which products and services can be developed in different circumstances and over time.

Basic Marketing
by Tom Cannon

The appeal of the strategies and portfolios approach lies in its ability to wed the underlying strength of strategic planning to the real-world limitations on management control in marketing today. The problems should not let us lose sight of the importance of strategy in allowing the firm to locate itself and its product in the marketplace. In this work, 'portfolio analysis' has emerged to play a central and important role. This approach has developed in a number of forms, but these have certain characteristics in common. The most critical of these is the notion that the products of the firm should be reviewed as if they represented a 'portfolio' of investment opportunities. A number of criteria can then be used to explore the nature of the investment opportunity, and the likely benefits and risks of expending additional funds and efforts to support the product to penetrate the market. The best known of the approaches to portfolio analysis is that employed by the Boston Consulting Group.

1 *Stars*
  These absorb considerable resources but have considerable potential for growth and profitability.
2 *Cash cows*
  These were probably 'stars' once, but there is now little growth in the market. They offer good returns now, but may have reached their peak.

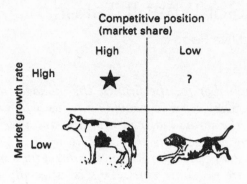

The business portfolio or growth share matrix

3 *Question marks*
'High growth, low share – have the worst characteristics of all.' They consume major resources but offer little prospect of good returns.
4 *Dogs*
These consume relatively little in the way of resources but offer little prospect of returns to the firm.

★

Dogbert's Rule of Strategies
**Any good strategy will seem ridiculous
by the time it is implemented.**

★

Murphy's Third Law
**In any field of endeavour, anything that can
go wrong will go wrong.**

Murphy's Fourth Law
**If there is a possibility of several things
going wrong, the one that will cause the most damage
will be the one to go wrong.**

Murphy's Fifth Law
If anything just cannot go wrong, it will anyway.

7 You Got What It Takes

The Competitive Edge

Strategies, whether for the firm or the manager, don't stand in isolation. They serve to provide a focus around which the business or the individual can mobilize resources to get an edge. Finding and refining this edge, using it to get ahead, is an ongoing struggle. Anita Roddick sums it up when she says that 'there are no short cuts'. This is especially true today. Serious rivals study the ways we succeed and strive to match and then overcome any advantage held earlier.

Anyone hoping to stay ahead has to show the same determination. Richard Branson brings out a crucial aspect of this when he talks about knowing the business areas in which you operate. This version of 'sticking to your last' means understanding past achievements but not being blinded by them. They are the platforms on which future successes will be built, but are no guarantee of continued prosperity.

John Kay's work has highlighted the link between the capabilities developed in the past – the rock on which success was built – and future accomplishments. The link lies in the distinctive capabilities of the firm which bring success when adapted to new conditions, applied in an industry and brought to a market. Orchestrating these capabilities to get and sustain an edge is an ongoing task. Those firms and managers that become especially skilled in this task have a massive advantage over their rivals which is summarized by Charles Revson's comment and the associated determination to win.

★

COMPETING

I don't meet competition. I crush it.
— *Charles Revson*

★

The nature of water is that it avoids heights
and hastens to the lowlands. When a dam is broken,
the water cascades with irresistible force.
Now the shape of an army resembles water.
Take advantage of the enemy's unpreparedness;
attack him when he does not expect it; avoid his strength
and strike his emptiness, and like water, none can oppose you.
— *Sun Tzu*

There is a story about two walkers in the Rocky Mountains. One morning they saw a giant mountain lion coming towards them down a narrow path. Immediately, one walker sat down and pulled a pair of running shoes from his back-pack. His colleague said in astonishment, 'You're crazy, you'll never outrun a mountain lion.' 'I know,' said his companion, 'but I'll sure as hell outrun you.'

In all business conditions, there are winners and losers. Anyone wanting to 'get ahead' must beat their rivals. Stiff local competition forced Japanese firms to develop the skills that eventually produced world-beating companies. Their success forces managers across the world to develop the same determination to win. Richard Branson highlights the importance of building from a secure base and getting involved in the struggle for competitive success.

The Decision Makers
by Robert Heller

It's a sobering thought (or should be) that it took the ferocious competition of the Japanese to make Western managements set off in search of 'competitive advantage'. Their lack of winning edge beforehand flowed from the inadequate level of prior striving, just as the winning ways of the Japanese sprang from their internecine battles back home. None of their internal trade wars was fiercer than the Honda–Yamaha struggle for supremacy in motorbikes, in which Yamaha went too far and awakened a sleeping giant. Knowing how far to go is a key piece of equipment for the decision-maker. Used properly, it can take him very far.

He won't, however, be likely to reach the perfect state of imperfect competition, in which there is no opposition worth mentioning. That was never easy without breaking the law. In

'You were warned not to muscle in on the expanded polystyrene market!'

modern times, monopoly has become a harder and harder game to play, because of the fragmentation of markets and the rapidity of change and challenge. Even great innovatory managements, like the SmithKline team which invented Tagamet or the EMI creators of computerised tomography (brain- and body-scanning), can fall foul of the laws of competition. The only protection lies not in protectionism, but perfectionism. The companies which sustain monopolistic market shares do so, paradoxically, by acting as if they were beset by formidable competitors on every side.

★

Wain's Ninth Conclusion
**People who mind their own business
succeed because they have
so little competition.**

★

'Risk Taking'
by Richard Branson

Know the business

The biggest risk any of us can take is to invest money in a business that we don't know. Very few of the businesses that Virgin has set up have been completely new fields. Admittedly, I started fresh – 'a virgin' – in the mail order record business, on the back of the abolition of retail price maintenance. Since then, however, the development of the Group has been through a linked series of investments, which I gather the business schools call vertical integration, but which I just call common sense. From the mail order business we went into retailing records, from the retailing of records we went into record production, through the setting up of the Virgin record label. We soon found that it was possible to negotiate music publishing rights as well as record rights with the same band, so we set up a music publishing company. Once we got past the very early stages, we realized that we were spending an awful lot of money on recording costs so we got into the recording studio business. When music videos became a necessary part of the marketing of records, we did not just make them and waste them, but began to distribute them ourselves. This got us into the video distribution business and it was a natural move to begin to acquire other products for video distribution. Another good example is when we noticed the increasing importance of film soundtracks; now it is almost worthwhile for us to get into a film for the soundtrack rights only. So behind the Richard Branson 'whizzkid, entrepreneur' image there lies – I believe – measured growth from the initial business of mail order through to the core of the Virgin Group as it is today.

- *So, know the business*
  These linkages do not happen without hard work and, in almost each case, I have devoted my time to the new business and have got completely immersed in it before making any significant investment.

  I have not depended upon others to do surveys, or a lot of market research, or to develop grand strategies. I have taken the view that the risk to the company is best reduced by my involvement in the nitty gritty of the new business.

- *So, get involved, don't stand back*
  That in turn means that I have got to depend a lot on the management of the divisions I leave behind when I become totally immersed in a new area. Risk management, which I suppose is what we are talking about, depends a lot on not risking your core business; and you do that by having a good management team in your core business before you embark on any risk venture in a new business. *So, don't depend* on others to do the diversification and to take the risk. *But do depend* on others to do the job they know.

The personal involvement highlighted in Richard Branson's piece ensures that those who understand the ways the firm adds and builds value take a lead in keeping the company ahead. Michael Porter's model of the value chain is a structured approach which helps managers understand the aspects of their firm that are special and distinct in the eyes of buyers. These assets can be successfully exploited to build loyalty and add new business. Peter Drucker warns against the complacency which often follows success.

Competitive Advantage
by Michael Porter

The value chain can be used as a strategic tool to analyse relative cost position, differentiation, and the role of competitive scope in achieving competitive advantage.

The value chain

Every firm is a collection of activities that are performed to design, produce, market, deliver, and support its product. All these activities can be represented using a value chain, shown in the figure overleaf. A firm's value chain and the way it performs individual activities are a reflection of its history, its strategy, its approach to implementing its strategy, and the underlying economics of the activities themselves.

Differences among competitor value chains are a key source of competitive advantage. A firm's value chain in an industry may vary somewhat for different items in its product line, or different buyers, geographic areas, or distribution channels. The value chains for such subsets of a firm are closely related, however, and can only be understood in the context of the business unit chain.

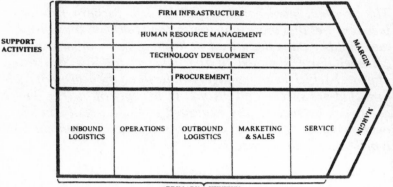

The generic value chain

★

Managing for Results
by Peter Drucker

Any leadership position is transitory and likely to be short-lived. No business is ever secure in its leadership position. The market in which the results exist, and the knowledge which is the resource, are both generally accessible. No leadership position is more than a temporary advantage. In business (as in a physical system) energy always tends towards diffusion. Business tends to drift from leadership to mediocrity. And the mediocre is three-quarters down the road to being marginal. Results always drift from earning a profit towards earning, at best, a fee which is all competence is worth.

It is, then, the executive's job to reverse the normal drift. It is his job to focus the business on opportunity and away from problems, to re-create leadership and counteract the trend towards mediocrity, to replace inertia and its momentum by new energy and new direction.

DISTINCTIVE STRENGTHS

John Kay of London Business School undertook the most authoritative recent study of competitive success in Europe. He warns against assuming that merely because features of the firm are distinctive, they can be sustained while adding value for customers against all rivals over time.

Foundations for Corporate Success
by John Kay

Sustainable and appropriate competitive advantage

A capability can only be distinctive if it is derived from a characteristic which other firms lack. Yet it is not enough for that characteristic to be distinctive. It is necessary also for it to be *sustainable* and *appropriable*. A distinctive capability is sustainable only if it persists over time. Honda's achievement was not only to redefine the US motorcycle market but to remain leaders in that market. A distinctive capability is appropriable only if it exclusively, or principally, benefits the company which holds it. Often the benefits of a distinctive capability are appropriated instead by employers, customers or by competitors.

There are relatively few types of distinctive capability which meet these conditions of sustainability and appropriability. There are three which recur in analysis of the performance of successful companies. *Innovation* is an obvious source of distinctive capability, but it is less often a sustainable or appropriable source because successful innovation quickly attracts imitation. Maintaining an advantage is most easily possible for those few innovations for which patent protection is effective. There are others where process secrecy or other characteristics make it difficult for other firms to follow. More often, turning an innovation into a competitive advantage requires the development of a powerful range of supporting strategies.

What appears to be competitive advantage derived from

innovation is frequently the return to a system of organization capable of producing a series of innovations. This is an example of a second distinctive capability which I call architecture. *Architecture* is a system of relationships within the firm, or between the firm and its suppliers and customers, or both. Generally, the system is a complex one and the content of the relationships implicit rather than explicit. The structure relies on continued mutual commitment to monitor and enforce its terms. A firm with distinctive architecture gains strength from the ability to transfer information which is specific to the firm, product or market within the organization and to its customers and suppliers. It can also respond quickly and flexibly to changing circumstances. It has often been through their greater ability to develop such architecture that Japanese firms have established competitive advantages over their American rivals.

A third distinctive capability is *reputation*. Reputation is, in a sense, a type of architecture but is so widespread and so important that it is best to treat it as a distinct source of competitive advantage. Easier to maintain than to create, reputation meets the essential conditions for sustainability. Indeed an important element of the strategy of many successful firms has been the transformation of an initial distinctive capability based on innovation or architecture to a more enduring one derived from reputation.

From capabilities to competitive advantages

A distinctive capability becomes a competitive advantage when it is *applied in an industry* and *brought to a market*. The market and the industry have both product and geographic dimensions. Sometimes the choice of market follows immediately from the nature of the distinctive capability. An innovation will usually suggest its own market. Pilkington discovered the float glass process, a system by which thin sheets of glass were formed on a bed of molten tin, which made the traditional grinding and polishing of plate glass unnecessary. Little need be said about the industry and markets where such an innovation is to be applied and it is other aspects of strategy that are critical. There are few geographical boundaries in innovation. While most innovating firms will begin in their home markets, successful innovation is rarely inhibited by national boundaries. The appropriate product market for an innovation is not always obvious, and identifying precisely what it is can be crucial. . . .

Other firms have distinctive capabilities based on their architecture, and the same architecture advantage can often be employed in a wide range of industries and markets. For BMW, the choice of industry and market segment was by no means obvious, but ultimately crucial. For Honda, the choice of market segment did seem obvious. In the wide open spaces of the United States, they anticipated little demand for the small machines which were popular in congested Japan. But this view was doubly wrong. The market for large bikes which they had chosen was one in which Honda had no initial competitive advantages. Success came only from a very different product positioning. . . .

Reputations are created in specific markets. A reputation necessarily relates to a product or a group of products. It is bounded geographically, too. Many reputations are very local in nature. The good plumber or doctor neither has nor needs a reputation outside a tightly defined area. Retailing reputations are mostly national. But an increasing number of producers of manufactured goods, from Coca-Cola to Sony, have established reputations world-wide, and branding has enabled international reputations to be created and exploited for locally delivered services in industries as diverse as accountancy and car hire.

A firm can only enjoy a competitive advantage relative to another firm in the same industry. So BMW may enjoy a competitive advantage over Nissan, but be at a competitive disadvantage to Mercedes. As this example illustrates, a competitive advantage is a feature of a particular market. These three firms compete in several different markets, or market segments, and the pattern of relative competitive advantages and disadvantages is different in each one. The value of a competitive advantage will depend on the strength of the firm's distinctive capability, the size of the market, and the overall profitability of the industry.

It is easier to sustain a distinctive capability in a narrow market than a wide one, more profitable to hold it in a wide market than a narrow one. And the profitability of a firm depends both on the competitive advantage the firm holds relative to other firms in the industry and on the profitability of the industry itself. If there is excess capacity in the industry – as in automobiles – then even a large competitive advantage may not yield substantial profits.

But if entry to an industry is difficult, then a firm without any competitive advantage may nevertheless earn very large returns. There is little reason to think that the large monopolistic utilities which control many parts of the European energy, transport, and communications industries have strong distinctive capabilities of the kind that characterize BMW, or Honda, or IBM. Their market dominance has not been built on doing things that others could not do as well, but on doing things that others were not permitted to do at all. Yet many of these firms are very profitable. There can be no greater competitive advantage than the absence of competitors. Profits come not only from distinctive capabilities but from possession of *strategic assets* – competitive advantages which arise from the structure of the market rather than from the specific attributes of firms within that market.

★

Next to knowing when to seize an opportunity,
the most important thing in life is to know
when to forego an advantage.
– *Benjamin Disraeli*

WINNING

Steiner's Philosophical Observations
**In business, as well as in chess, the winner is
the one who makes the next to last mistake.**

★

★

**If there is a single characteristic which is found in
all our successful companies, in most cases to an outstanding
degree, it is the overwhelming commitment to winning.**
– The Winning Streak *by W. Goldsmith & D. Clutterbuck*

*John Kay's earlier piece on the constant struggle to stay ahead
brings out a key difference between business and many other
areas of competitive activity. There are no gold medals, just a
temporary advantage over rivals determined to steal your best
ideas and introduce some of their own. No one shows this
determination to get ahead and stay there more clearly than
Alan Sugar in the piece that follows.*

Alan Sugar: The Amstrad Story
by Alan Sugar

Yet Sugar displayed no sign of throttling back or of taking it easy. On the contrary, friends of his from that time describe an intense man, preoccupied with succeeding in his business to the exclusion of everything else. He confided in one friend that the demands of running his business on his own used to keep him awake at night. He had a compulsion to win which was quite out of the ordinary, as one old friend relates: 'If you sat down and played a game with him, if he wasn't winning, he played till two or three o'clock in the morning till he *was* winning. He was like a bear with a sore head if he didn't win. He wanted to prove something all the time to everybody.'

Alan Sugar strains every sinew to keep winning. His survival in the Information Technology sector has forced him to accept Devereux's Conjecture that 'Today's success is tomorrow's liability'. This time pressure on modern firms is producing a new and vital source of competitive advantage. George Stalk and Thomas Hout – top managers at the Boston Consulting Group – have reshaped thinking about the way firms compete by drawing out the ways they can use time to get ahead.

Competing Against Time
by George Stalk Jr. & Thomas M. Hout

Wal-Mart is one of the fastest growing retailers in the United States. Its stores move nearly $20 billion of merchandise a year. Only K Mart and the floundering giant, Sears, are larger. Wal-Mart's success is due to many factors not the least of which is responsiveness. Wal-Mart replenishes the stock in its stores on average twice a week. Many stores receive deliveries daily. The typical competitor – K Mart, Sears, or Zayre –

replenishes its stock every two weeks. Compared to these competitors, Wal-Mart can

- Maintain the same service levels with one-fourth the inventory investment.
- Offer its customers four times the choice of stock for the same investment in inventory.
- Do some of both.

Wal-Mart is growing three times faster than the retail discount industry as a whole and has a return on capital that is more than twice as high as the industry average.

Atlas Door is now the leading supplier of industrial overhead doors in the United States. Atlas can fill an order for an out-of-stock door in three to four weeks, one-third the industry average.

Customers are rewarding Atlas Door's responsiveness by buying most of their doors from them, often at 20 per cent price premiums. Wilson promises to manufacture and deliver the desired product in ten days or less. Some competitors need more than 30 days to respond to an out-of-stock situation. Demand for WilsonArt decorative laminates is growing three times faster than overall demand, and the profitability of Ralph Wilson Plastics is four times greater than that of the average competitor.

Thomasville Furniture is a new breed of competitor in a US industry plagued by slow and unreliable suppliers. Thomasville has a quick-ship programme. A buyer is promised 30-day delivery if the article desired is not in stock at the company stores. The average industry response to a similar out-of-stock situation is longer than three months. Thomasville is growing four times faster than the industry, and the company is twice as profitable as the US industry average.

Citicorp introduced MortgagePower three years ago. It promised the buyer and the realtor a loan commitment in fifteen days or less. The typical loan originator requires 30 to 60 days to make a commitment. Demand for Citicorp's mortgage loans is growing more than 100 per cent per year in an industry with an average growth of 3 per cent per year.

Clearly, the time advantage is enabling time-based competitors to upset the traditional leaders of their industries and to claim the number one competitive and profitability positions. When a time-based competitor can open up a response advantage with turnaround times three to four times faster than its competitors, it will almost always grow three times faster than the average for the industry and will be twice as profitable as the average for all competitors. Moreover, these estimates are 'floors.' Many time-based competitors grow faster and earn even higher profits relative to their competitors.

DIFFERENTIATION

All the firms identified by Stalk and Hout distinguish themselves from their rivals and put competitors at a disadvantage by giving customers what they want when they want it. This distinguishes them from their rivals. Michael Porter shows how this advantage starts with the customer and ends at the centre of the firm's operations. The sheer joy of winning – especially against an entrenched rival – is captured by John Sculley when he describes the scene at PepsiCo's HQ. For Kendall, who had joined Pepsi as a fountain syrup salesman in 1947, the success was especially sweet. Richard Dawkins shows how this desire to survive and succeed is deeply rooted in human nature.

Competitive Advantage
by Michael Porter

Steps in differentiation

1 Determine who the real buyer is.
2 Identify the buyer's value chain and the firm's impact on it.
3 Determine ranked buyer purchasing criteria.

4 Assess the existing and potential sources of uniqueness in a firm's value chain.

5 Identify the cost of existing and potential sources of differentiation.

6 Choose the configuration of value activities that creates the most valuable differentiation for the buyer relative to cost of differentiating.

7 Test the chosen differentiation strategy for sustainability.

8 Reduce cost in activities that do not affect the chosen forms of differentiation.

★

Odyssey: From Pepsi to Apple
by John Sculley

Clouds of smoke, even laughter, engulfed the room as the figures revealed an achievement it had taken nearly a decade to create: Pepsi had surpassed Coke in sales as the leading soft drink sold in the nation's supermarkets.

'This is what I've longed for during my entire career,' Kendall exulted, 'to beat Coke fair and square.'

Finally, in the spring of 1978, Pepsi was number one, the leading revenue producer of the more than 20,000 items sold in a supermarket – the freedom-of-choice market. The Nielsens proved it. The numbers on the screen showed that we had captured a 30.8 per cent share of the national market to Coke's 29.2 per cent, a slice of business worth more than $3 billion. We had inched ahead of Coke in some bimonthly periods a year earlier, but now we could claim a clear, unshakable full-year victory.

It was one of those moments for which you worked your entire career. We always believed, since the early seventies, when Pepsi was widely viewed as the perennial also-ran, that we could do it. All of us started out with that objective, and we never took our eyes off it.

My fixation on this goal surfaced as soon as I joined the company as a trainee in 1967. My success, my reputation as a marketing wizard, all were dependent on the Nielsens and this race to gain the seven share points – some $700 million in additional sales – that would put us over the top. I became at the age of thirty Pepsi's youngest marketing vice president in 1970, when I began to speak publicly about how we were going to dethrone Coke. Most people, including our own bottlers, thought we were crazy. But Coke was a little like the Wizard of Oz – so powerful was its image that few foresaw that the company was vulnerable to attack by new ideas. Seven years later, partly on the basis of those ideas, I was named the youngest Pepsi-Cola president.

If I was brash or arrogant on my way to the top, it mattered little to me. I was an impatient perfectionist. I was willing to work relentlessly to get things exactly right. I was unsympathetic to those who couldn't deliver the results I demanded. I was driven, not by simple power or raw ambition, but by an insatiable curiosity and scepticism as to business's accepted notions. I considered myself a builder, someone whose success was dependent on building products and markets, on changing an industry's ground rules, not merely competing. I felt as if I were an architect of new ideas and concepts. Yet I was happy to meet the tests of competition, and at Pepsi they appeared frequently.

★

The Selfish Gene
by Richard Dawkins

The logical policy for a survival machine might therefore seem to be to murder its rivals, and then, preferably, to eat them. Although murder and cannibalism do occur in nature, they are not as common as a naïve interpretation of the selfish gene theory might predict. Indeed Konrad Lorenz, in *On Aggression*, stresses the restrained and gentlemanly nature of animal fighting. For him the notable thing about animal fights is that they are formal tournaments, played according to rules like those of boxing or fencing. Animals fight with gloved fists and blunted foils. Threat and bluff take the place of deadly earnest. Gestures of surrender are recognized by victors, who then refrain from dealing the killing blow or bite which our naïve theory might predict.

This interpretation of animal aggression as being restrained and formal can be disputed. In particular, it is certainly wrong to condemn poor old *Homo sapiens* as the only species to kill his own kind, the only inheritor of the mark of Cain, and similar melodramatic charges. Whether a naturalist stresses the violence or the restraint of animal aggression depends partly on the kinds of animals he is used to watching, and partly on his evolutionary preconceptions – Lorenz is, after all, a 'good of the species' man. Even if it has been exaggerated, the gloved fist view of animal fights seems to have at least some truth. Superficially this looks like a form of altruism. The selfish gene theory must face up to the difficult task of explaining it. Why is it that animals do not go all out to kill rival members of their species at every possible opportunity?

The general answer to this is that there are costs as well as benefits resulting from outright pugnacity, and not only the obvious costs in time and energy. For instance, suppose that B and C are both my rivals, and I happen to meet B. It might seem sensible for me as a selfish individual to try to kill him. But wait. C is also my rival, and C is also B's rival. By killing B, I am potentially doing a good turn to C by removing one of his rivals. I might have done better to let B live, because he might then have competed or fought with C, thereby benefiting me indirectly. The moral of this simple hypothetical example is that there is no obvious merit in indiscriminately trying to kill rivals. In a large and complex system of rivalries, removing one rival from the scene does not necessarily do any good: other rivals may be more likely to benefit from his death than oneself. This is the kind of hard lesson that has been learned by pest-control officers. You have a serious agricultural pest, you discover a good way to exterminate it and you gleefully do so, only to find that another pest benefits from the extermination even more than human agriculture does, and you end up worse off than you were before.

On the other hand, it might seem a good plan to kill, or at least fight with, certain particular rivals in a discriminating way. If B is an elephant seal in possession of a large harem full of females, and if I, another elephant seal, can acquire his harem by killing him, I might be well advised to attempt to do so. But there are costs and risks even in selectivity pugnacity. It is to B's advantage to fight back, to defend his valuable property. If I start a fight, I am just as likely to end up dead as he is. Perhaps even more so. He holds a valuable resource, that is why I want to fight him. But why does he hold it? Perhaps he won it in combat. He has probably beaten off other challengers before me. He is probably a good fighter. Even if I win the fight and gain the harem, I may be so badly mauled in the process that I cannot enjoy the benefits. Also, fighting uses up time and energy. These might be better conserved for the time being. If I concentrate on feeding and on keeping out of trouble for a time, I shall grow bigger and stronger. I'll fight him for the harem in the end, but I may have a better chance of winning eventually if I wait, rather than rush in now.

This subjective soliloquy is just a way of pointing out that the decision whether or not to fight should ideally be preceded by a complex, if unconscious, 'cost-benefit' calculation. The potential benefits are not all stacked up on the side of fighting, although undoubtedly some of them are. Similarly, during a fight, each tactical decision over whether to escalate the fight or cool it has costs and benefits which could, in principle, be analysed.

★

Field's First Law of Success
If at first you don't succeed, try, try again.
Then quit. No use being a damn fool about it.

8 I've Gotta Getta Message to You

Marketing, Advertising and Sales

Charles Revson has shown in some well-known comments why his companies have succeeded in being customer driven. When he said, 'In our factories we make perfumes, in our markets we sell dreams,' he understood that his customers did not want to buy products, they wanted to satisfy needs. A specific product or service succeeded or failed because it met these needs at a moment in time, for particular groups of customers. The priority for the customer-driven business is to continually mould itself, its products and services around the needs of its customers. This requires particular sets of skills and a clear focus on the market.

Stew Leonard shows how this means going beyond any individual transaction to a deeper understanding of the long-term relationship between the firm and its customers. His company motto puts this well:

> Rule 1: *The Customer is Always Right*
> Rule 2: *If the Customer is Ever Wrong, Read Rule 1*

Without this type of vision and perspective it is hard to build a customer-driven organisation. The promise cannot be delivered without the systematic application of some basic disciplines. These include regular market research, ongoing efforts to improve standards and performance and, perhaps most of all, a basic respect for those who buy your products and use your services.

★

Marketing is human activity directed at satisfying needs and wants through exchange processes.
– Marketing Management *by Philip Kotler*

THE TASK

The discussion about strategy and competitiveness in Chapter 7 emphasized the importance of meeting customer needs. In most organizations, the sales and marketing team provide the cutting edge to the effort to satisfy these requirements. Philip Kotler – the doyen of marketing writers – spells out the kinds of skills and attributes required by the successful marketer. These specialist skills can only work if, as Tom Peters points out, everyone in the firm appreciates the value of a customer and the cost of losing their support. Supplier attitudes would soon change if they realized just how much a loyal customer brings in during a lifetime of support.

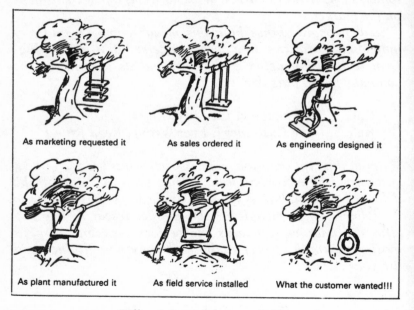

As marketing requested it	As sales ordered it	As engineering designed it
As plant manufactured it	As field service installed	What the customer wanted!!!

Different views of the same problem

'From Sales Obsession to Marketing Effectiveness'
by Philip Kotler

Job of the marketing executive

What is the proper conception of the job of a high-level marketing executive? The answer has gone through three stages of thinking.

The earliest and most popular view is that the marketing executive is an expert at *demand stimulation*. He or she is someone who knows how to combine the tools of marketing to create an efficient impact on chosen markets. The marketing executive understands buyers' wants, buying influences, channels, and competition, and is able to use product features, personal selling, advertising, sales promotion, price, and service to stimulate purchasing behaviour.

More recently, a broader conception of the marketing executive has been proposed: he should be an expert in *demand management*. The marketing executive works with a varied and changing set of demand problems. Sometimes demand is too low and must be stimulated, sometimes demand is too irregular and must be evened out or 'smoothed', sometimes demand is temporarily too high (as in a shortage period) and must be reduced with 'de-marketing.'

The increasingly volatile state of the economy is one reason that the marketing executive needs broad skills in demand management rather than abilities only in demand stimulation. The varying fortunes of different company divisions is another reason. Every multidivision company has certain divisions whose low sales growth, market share, or profitability may call for a strategic objective other than growth. The strategic objective might be to maintain, 'harvest', or terminate sales. Hence the marketing executive must be skilled at more tasks than simply stimulating demand.

★

'. . . then we lost the Andrex account.'

★

Thriving on Chaos
by Tom Peters

Treat the customer as an appreciating asset

When the Federal Express courier enters my office, she should see '$180,000' stamped on the forehead of our receptionist. My little twenty-five-person firm runs about a $1,500-a-month Fed Ex bill. Over ten years, that will add up to $180,000. I suggest that this simple device, calculating the ten-year (or, alternatively, lifetime) value of a customer can be very powerful – and has sweeping implications.

Grocer Stew Leonard got me started on this. He says, 'When I see a frown on a customer's face, I see $50,000 about to walk out the door.' His good customers buy about $100 worth of groceries a week. Over ten years, that adds up to roughly $50,000. We all agree that repeat trade is the key to business success. This simple quantifying device provides a way to add potency to the idea.

Here are two other examples. Average lifetime auto purchases will total about $150,000, not including repair work. Given the remarkable low dealer loyalty of car buyers these days, might it not make a difference if dealers and their employees focused on this big number? Or suppose you frequent a good restaurant twice a month for a six-person business dinner. You're worth about $75,000 every ten years to that establishment.

Imposing as they are, these figures are just the tip of the iceberg. The repeat customer is also any firm's principal vehicle for powerful word-of-mouth advertising. Conservatively, suppose a lifelong, happy customer sells just one colleague on becoming a lifelong customer of your fine restaurant, grocery store, or Federal Express, as the case may be. Suddenly, the regular customer's value to the restaurant doubles from $75,000 to $150,000, including that likely word-of-mouth referral. And that sign on my receptionist's forehead should now be read by the Fed Ex person as $360,000 rather than $180,000.

There's a third step in the progression. If the restaurant's waiter handles five tables a night, he or she is catering to 5 × $150,000, or $750,000, worth of potential business. The numbers are stunning for Fed Ex. If our courier has forty each day, this is a 'portfolio' of customers worth 40 × $360,000, or $14 million, to Federal Express!

So the three-step formula is: First, estimate the ten-year or lifelong value of a customer, based upon the size and frequency of a good customer's average transaction. Then multiply that number by two, to take into account the word-of-mouth factor. Finally, multiply the new total by the average number of customers served per day by the sales, service, dispatch, or other front-line person or group. The result is the lifelong value of the 'customer portfolio' that that individual or group deals with each day.

The implication is clear: *If you look at customers in this or a related way, you are likely to take a new view of hiring, training, compensating, and spending on tools to aid the customer-serving process.* Take that waiter, managing $750,000 of your future each night. Are you still sure you want to brag about the low average wages you pay? Are you certain that skimping on uniform quality makes sense? Does the investment in a small computer system to support order taking still look as expensive as it did? Suddenly, Stew Leonard's insistence that everyone in the store go through the lengthy Dale Carnegie public-speaking and attitude courses is seen in a different light. So is the high pay at Federal Express, and its seemingly lavish spending on support tools, such as the Cosmos computer system that soon will include a terminal in each delivery truck. (On the reverse side, it makes the failure of People Express to invest in service support tools incomprehensible.)

CUSTOMER RELATIONS

The Manager's Handbook *provides an invaluable checklist for anyone seeking to assess their current efforts. But checklists are only a starting point. The key to success, as Tom Peters points out, is making sure that everyone in the firm is listening to customers and is determined to respond to their needs.*

The Manager's Handbook
by Arthur Young

The end product of marketing

To achieve the right mix of products and markets for the company and its customers, you need to:

● Analyse opportunities by asking: Who needs our products? What are our strengths? What are our customer needs?

- Select realistic objectives by using a consistent background for decision-making and planning. Then define roles and provide a sense of purpose.
- Develop strategy by recognizing internal strengths and weaknesses and external opportunities and threats. Develop tactics to beat the opposition.
- Formulate plans by drawing up your game plan according to resources.
- Implement and control: make it happen.

Good customer relations are essential for the success of a business. They are achieved by:

- Good customer service.
- Product margins which meet the company's objectives and give the customer value for money.
- Relevant product development and innovation to meet customers' future needs.
- Regular sales calls and entertainment proportional to sales potential.

Too good customer relations can mean:

- Service costs too high.
- Margins too low.
- High development costs of products with limited markets.
- Late payments.
- Too many sales calls.
- High entertainment costs.

Bad customer relations are due to:

- Poor service.
- Products seen as poor value for money.
- No interest in customers' future needs.
- Insensitive credit control procedures.

- Infrequent sales calls.
- Low entertainment costs.

If the balance swings too heavily in either direction, the result is *loss of profit.*

★

'Listen, mate, you think I enjoy being lumbered with the tequila promotion?'

★

Thriving on Chaos
by Tom Peters

Involve everyone in customer listening

If intensity and rapid feedback are the most important aspects of real listening, the involvement of everyone in the process follows closely. Customer listening is not just a marketing, sales, and service job. At one end of the spectrum, every clerk and machine operator should be involved. At the other end, the ivory tower researcher should also be thrown into the fray. A very high-tech firm finally cajoled its top R&D person, who epitomized the 'what can I learn from these jerks' mentality, into visiting customers. He got very excited, and the president took advantage of his reaction by pushing him in front of a video camera to extol the virtues of getting out and about with customers. The tape is played in every training session.

Use every listening post you can find

One important point, then, is not to leave listening and market research to the experts. Another deals with what constitutes 'good listening.' The answer is clear: any angle you can dream up. One highly successful banker is an avid reader of local banking newsletters from around the country. He's an avowed thief. In his fast-paced world, new products are being introduced daily. He reads voraciously to get the first scent of anything that he might copy. And while he has a talented marketing department, by setting an example through his ceaseless circulation of little titbits about this and that, he encourages everyone to get attuned to doing his or her own listening/'market research.'

ACTION

It is the will to act on the insights gained from listening to customers that separate the successful from the unsuccessful marketer. Turning these insights into action calls for an understanding of the way advertising, promotion and selling works.

'Keeping Informed: Clues for Advertising Strategists'
by D. F. Cox

In order for an audience to be influenced in the desired manner by a communication, several conditions must be met:

- The audience must, somehow, be *exposed* to the communication
- Members of the audience must interpret or *perceive* correctly what action or attitude is desired of them by the communicator.
- The audience must remember or *retain* the gist of the message that the communicator is trying to get across.
- Members of the audience must *decide* whether or not they will be influenced by the communication.

★

'It doesn't seem the same since the sponsorship deal.'

The Manager's Handbook
by Arthur Young

Selling

Management is fundamentally about direction and control. Selling is no different.

All salespeople, particularly those in large companies, present a basic problem: they enjoy spending their time doing what they know best, with the products that are easiest to sell, and selling to those customers who are easiest to sell to. Direction, management and control are needed to ensure that selling time and cost is spent where it is most effective – on prime and hot prospects.

Successful sales managers and directors keep the pressure on their sales force by meeting regularly with them to review:

- Performance versus budget.
- Key performance ratios.
- Follow-up procedures.
- Opportunities.
- Competitor activity.

Incentives do not figure high on this list. Many sales managers spend too much time inventing elaborate sales incentive schemes, which the salesforce can manipulate to their personal benefit. Incentives must be geared toward the overall objectives of the marketing plan in terms of turnover and cost. When used, they should be short, sharp and regular, enhancing the overall sales effort, *not* detracting from it.

Sales incentive schemes are often an excuse for poor management of the sales resource. There are many lasting benefits in creating an effective team relationship within a sales force: shared experience is a benefit that does not arise from a totally competitive environment.

The other forgotten standard of performance is control of debt. A sale is not a sale until the debt has been paid. The sales force should chase up money owed to the company. It was responsible for the sale and should be responsible for assessing its payment – before team members are paid a bonus.

How well are we doing?

The key performance indicators of selling activity are:

Ratios
- Percentage sales: budget.
- Contract/orders: quotations.
- Quotations: leads.
- Percentage margins: sales.

Salesforce
- Number of calls.
- Number of new prospects called/found.
- Progress on enquiries/quotations.
- Credit control (age debt of sales).
- Frequency of calls per day/week/month etc.
- Length of calls.
- Percentage discounts: sales overall utilization.
- Number of customers and their value.
- Administration of sales reports/prospects.
- Submission of itineraries.

Overall
- Cost of sales force/sales.
- Sales value/order.
- Orders to calls ratio.
- Percentage discounts: sales.
- Key account development.

Know your customer base. It may be most appropriate to spend 80 per cent of your selling/promotional activity with 20 per cent of your clients who account for 80 per cent of your turnover.

One of the most positive developments of recent years in marketing is renewed attention to the vital role of sales staff. Their 'heroics' can often have a more marked effect on the bottom line than the cleverest advertising and the most scientific research.

Thriving on Chaos
by Tom Peters

A strategy for inducing sales and service force heroics

There are at least nine critical factors for enhancing attention to sales, service, and support people:

1 Spend time with them.
2 Pay them well.
3 Recognize them.
4 Listen to them.
5 Make sales and service a feeder route to general management.
6 Empower them.
7 Train them.
8 Support them technically.
9 Hire enough of them!

COMMITMENT

The success of the best sales staff often comes from their deep commitment to the company, its products and services. This commitment needs to permeate the entire company if the firm wants to be customer driven. Anita Roddick shows how this can be achieved when everyone inside the firm shares a vision which can be extended to include customers and suppliers. This is close to Richard's Rule which states that 'The value we add comes from the values we hold.'

'What is Customer-Driven Marketing?'
by J. Naumann

What is 'customer driven'?

Being customer driven is much like motherhood and apple pie; it's hard to argue against. However, many firms – indeed, most firms – are not really customer driven, if their actions offer any indication. Too many firms take their customers for granted and make only superficial efforts to satisfy them. For a firm to become truly customer driven, a major shift in corporate philosophy must exist. Such a change in orientation usually results from a gradual, evolutionary process.

It appears there are at least three stages through which a firm must pass to become truly customer driven: (1) bliss, (2) awareness, and (3) commitment. A firm finds itself in one of these evolutionary stages of development based on performance, not on desire. Having a CEO say 'we're customer oriented' is meaningless unless the statement is backed up by real programmes.

● *Bliss*
There is an old adage that 'ignorance is bliss.' Many firms are blissful, indeed. The management of the 'blissful' firm feels it produces a good product because it often has a good finished-product quality-control programme. It has reasonable warranties and tries to treat its customers fairly. Very often the firm will have a lenient return or exchange policy for its products. After all, the blissful firm wants to keep its customers satisfied! The blissful firm often has a customer service department that handles customer complaints. When a customer misuses or abuses a product, the blissful firm will allow the customer at least partial credit, although, as its managers will tell you when you ask, it doesn't really have to.

So what is wrong with the blissful firm? The problem is that this firm is in a reactive, status quo mode. It uses its customer service department to react to customer complaints, most likely without realizing that typically fewer than 5 per cent of dissatisfied customers actually complain to the company itself. The blissful firm does not understand that the cost of acquiring a new customer can be as much as five times the cost of keeping an existing one. The blissful firm is comfortable with its current operation and has not established an environment for continual innovation and improvements. . . .

- *Awareness*

The second level in the transition toward customer orientation is awareness that customer satisfaction is important. An aware firm has all of the characteristics of a blissful firm but is more proactive. Whereas both blissful and aware firms say that customers are important, aware firms actually implement practices that indicate they mean it.

Aware firms have customer service departments, as do blissful firms, but aware firms will open customer service departments for extended hours to make it easier for customers to use the service. They provide toll-free calling; they may have a bilingual customer service staff.

In addition to these reactive measures, the aware firm takes such proactive steps as conditioning regularly scheduled customer satisfaction surveys. The most aware firms design customer surveys to measure what customers actually think. This is in direct opposition to non-aware firms, who obtain only the information the firm wants to hear. The marketing managers of aware firms pay attention to the results of surveys and use the information to help the organization improve its products and services. . . .

- *Commitment*

Committed firms realize that achieving customer satisfaction cannot result from just doing the traditional things better. Good product quality warranties, and customer surveys can help, but they are inadequate without something more. The 'something' is changing the customer from a target to a partner.

As a partner, the customer is actually involved in a firm's decision-making processes at many levels in the organization. Committed firms recognize that customers are a valuable asset and a source of innovation. Therefore, committed firms actively develop mechanisms for customer involvement comprehensively throughout the firm.

★

Body and Soul
by Anita Roddick

Our values were diametrically opposed to the business practices of the cosmetics industry in just about every area:

- They were prepared to sell false hopes and unattainable dreams; I was not. From the start, we explained to customers in simple language everyone could understand exactly what a product would do and what it wouldn't do.
- They sold through hype; I was so innocent I didn't even know what hype was.
- They thought packaging was important; I thought it was totally irrelevant. We happily filled old lemonade bottles with our products if a customer asked.
- They tested on animals; I was repulsed by the practice and made it clear that I would never sell a product that had been tested on animals.
- They spent millions on market research; we simply said to our customers, 'Tell us what you want and we will try and get it for you.'
- They all had huge marketing departments; I never fully understood what marketing was.
- They had enormous advertising budgets; we have never spent a cent on advertising. At the beginning we couldn't afford it, and by the time we could afford it we had got to the point where I would be too embarrassed to do it.

- They talked about beauty products; I banished the word 'beauty'.
- They worshipped profits; we didn't. In all the time I have been in business we have never had a meeting to discuss profits – we wouldn't know how to do it.
- Finally, and most importantly, they thought it was not the business of business to get involved in wider issues, in the protection of the environment or involvement with the community; I thought there was nothing more important.

★

Robbin's Rules of Marketing

1 Your share of the market is really lower than you think.
2 Never delay the end of a meeting or the beginning of a cocktail hour.
3 The combined market position goals of all competitors always totals at least 150 per cent.
4 The existence of a market does not ensure the existence of a customer.
5 Strategies develop most easily from big backlogs.
6 Beware of alleged needs that have no real market.
7 The worth of a thing is what it will bring.
8 Low price and long shipment will win over high price and short shipment.
9 Umbrella pricing encourages noncompetitive costs.
10 The competition really can have lower prices.
11 If you can't get the whole job, settle for part of it.
12 The number of competitors never declines.
13 Secret negotiations are usually neither.
14 A good presentation has as many questions as answers.
15 If the customer wants vanilla, give him vanilla.
16 If the customer buys lunch, you've lost the order.
17 Unless constantly nurtured, nothing is as short-lived as a good customer.
18 No matter how good the deal, the customer is always sceptical.

9 Speak to Me Pretty

Communication and Negotiation

I have never been in a company facing problems and struggling to survive without finding serious communication problems. Often, the managers involved suggest that these communication problems are symptoms of the wider problems:

> *'We don't want to alarm people by telling them too much.'*
> *'We don't want to worry staff.'*
> *'Our best staff will leave if we tell them anything about the problems facing us.'*

These phrases could stand as epitaphs to a host of companies and careers. Keeping people in the dark feeds rumours and increases fears. Your best people are the very people who will get the firm out of its troubles – if they get the chance.

Poor communication is more often a cause of difficulties than a symptom. More managers talk about the importance of communication than take any serious steps to communicate effectively with their colleagues. This criticism often provokes replies like 'I am always telling my staff what is happening,' or 'I send out frequent memos.' Sadly many of these managers do not understand the difference between transmission and communication. The latter does not occur until the recipient has received and understood the message.

★

MESSAGES

★

Lewis' Lament
When all is said and done, there's more said than done.

The strongest temptation in communication is to assume that because I've said something in terms I understand, those I want to reach will understand it equally. Louis Boone highlights this in his anecdote about the plumber.

Quotable Business
by Louis E. Boone

In his book *The Power of Words*, Stuart Chase emphasized the value of the KISS ('Keep it simple, stupid') approach to effective communications by telling the story of the plumber who decided to use hydrochloric acid to clean drains but became concerned about possible harmful effects. His letter to the US Bureau of Standards in Washington, DC, produced this reply:

The efficacy of hydrochloric acid is indisputable, but chlorine residue is incompatible with metallic permanence.

The plumber read the letter and then sent a follow-up letter to his correspondent in Washington, thanking him for responding and expressing his satisfaction in learning that his practice was a safe one. He received a brief note of alarm by return mail:

We cannot assume responsibility for the production of toxic and noxious residues with hydrochloric acid, and suggest that you use an alternative procedure.

Again, the plumber responded expressing his pleasure at the fact that the bureau still agreed with him. This produced an even briefer, more direct note from Washington:

Don't use hydrochloric acid; it eats hell out of the pipes.

★

Message to deep-sea diver:
'Surface at once. Ship is sinking.'

METHODS OF COMMUNICATION

The problems of the plumber above would disappear if organizations like the US Bureau of Standards put themselves in the shoes of the listener. The steps described by Francis and Heather Kelly – based on their experience at Harvard Business School – are an invaluable starting point for effective communication. Central to their approach is the notion that communication is a two-way process with the message received as important as the message sent.

What They Really Teach You
at the Harvard Business School
by Francis J. Kelly & Heather M. Kelly

The importance of effective management communication

Effective management communication has always been important in business, but as we move into a world that is increasingly media-intensive, effective communication skills are
becoming even more important. . . .

Select the message clearly

One technique many HBSers find useful in class and on the job
after graduation is to jot down an outline of one, two, or maybe
three topics that absolutely must be covered in an up-coming
phone call or meeting, and to mentally rehearse before beginning to speak.

Given the goal of knowing exactly what to say, HBS students
pursue a four-step process to select the best possible message
for any given situation.

1 Consider the situation and determine what all the possible
  communication options are. Should one go into great
  detail or little? How much background should be given?
  Should one make a recommendation or not? How strongly
  should one come across? Should one speak now or wait a
  day or a week, or maybe not respond at all? To whom
  should the message be directed? Are there others one
  should communicate with?
2 Stand back from the options developed and ask, What is it
  that really *must* be said?
3 The third step comes quickly on top of the second. Ask,
  What should be said, given the politics and the
  personalities involved? In some MC cases it seemed clear
  that saying less was better. Other times, the situation being

examined demanded that questions be answered to ensure that all parties could move on to the appropriate next steps.

4 Determine exactly how to convey the message determined to be correct based on steps one through three. Should it be done in a phone call, a letter, or in a face-to-face meeting? Which exact words and tone of voice should be used?

Every student's work in MC is thoroughly evaluated by the class instructor and by one or more fellow students. The advice stressed over and over again includes the following recommendations:

- Use words carefully; say exactly what is intended.
- Be concise.
- Tailor language and style to fit the audience.
- Be very clear about the actions one wishes others to take.
- If assertions are made, include clear support for them.
- Anticipate questions and answer them (before they're asked) in the initial communication. This saves time and increases persuasiveness.

The last point is particularly important. More often than not, one can't order people to do things in the business world. One must persuade them to act according to one's wishes. The more effectively communication – whether written, or spoken over the phone or in person – is able to answer all conceivable questions, the more likely the person or persons being addressed will be able to respond favourably.

★

★

Enterprise
by Tom Cannon

Communication

The task of those wishing to manage communication more effectively lies in structuring and organising *signals* to achieve their desired ends. These are just four communication channels: visual (sight), auditory (sound), olfactory (smell) and tactile (touch). Each can be used to create an impression. The salesman passes material around his audience to reassure them of its quality. The restaurateur has smells coming from the kitchen as the menu is read. In the vast majority of institutional contexts visual and auditory channels dominate. Managing these is the primary task of the communicator.

Creating the right environment is an important first step. This should minimize negative bias and gain the greatest benefit for the message. Negative bias can come from several sources. The appearance of the individual transmitting the message has a marked effect. This should reassure the audience and add credibility to the message. Eye contact establishes a bridge between those taking part. The physiology matters. There are limits on the amount of information that can be absorbed. This is reduced by lack of trust, emotion and distance.

The presentation
The underlying rule that communication is centred on the receivers focuses attention on *their* objectives. The presentation which does not address the issues which concern clients in terms they understand will not succeed. The manager who talks to workers about a change in work practice and leaves them with the wrong impression has failed. The way the audience receives and interprets the message is more important than the manner in which it is sent. The rules which guide the formal presentation illustrate many of the principles which underlie all effective communication. These are:

1 Specify the message to be sent.
2 Define the audience.
3 Adjust the message to the capabilities of the audience.
4 Review the medium employed.
5 Fit the message to the medium.
6 Design presentation for clarity.
7 Reinforce verbal with visual signals.
8 Provide opportunities for feedback.

★

Davidson's Law of Inquiry
People ask stupid questions for a reason.

POINTS OF VIEW

Conventional thinking often starts from the absurd assumption that the listener is a passive object merely waiting to hear and absorb the message. Tom Peters vividly illustrates the active contribution to effective communication which is made by the listeners. Once an active, two-way view is taken, the scope for building successful communication extends dramatically. The Manager's Handbook *highlights some of the alternative routes open to communicators who concentrate on getting the message across, even in the type of crisis identified by David Bernstein.*

Thriving on Chaos
by Tom Peters

Make listening fun

Listening can even be fun! That's the point of the VPI, or Very Promotable Item. Wal-Mart Stores' growth has been phenomenal, from $50 million per year in sales to over $15 billion in just fifteen years; from 15 to 1,000 stores in that same period. Now, in 99 out of 100 cases of such growth, executive detachment from the market follows – detachment in which lie the seeds of eventual decline. Wal-Mart, however, led by the indomitable Sam Walton, has battled the negative side effects of growth as successfully as any company I know. Executives, including Sam himself, are regularly out and about with their customers. The terrible 'Taj Mahal phenomenon' has not set in: Wal-Mart's 'headquarters' in Bentonville, Arkansas, are every bit as spartan as they were a decade ago.

Of all Wal-Mart's defences against hardening of the corporate arteries, though, the VPI is my favourite. Each of the top executives (and, as of 1985, their spouses) picks out an item of store merchandise that he or she will directly sponsor throughout the year. For instance, Sam (who chooses three items instead of one in deference to his position) selected a five-gallon plastic fisherman's bait bucket in 1985. He was responsible for tracking its progress throughout the year, for pushing store managers to merchandise it aggressively, for giving those managers ideas about how to display and price the item, and for keeping tabs on it whenever he's in a store.

★

Farr's Law of Mean Familiarity
**This can be expressed as a curve,
but is much clearer set down as follows:**
The Guv'nor addresses:

Co-director Michael Yates as *Mike*;
Assistant director Michael Yates as *Michael*;
Section manager Michael Yates as *Mr Yates*;
Second assistant Michael Yates as *Yates*;
Apprentice Michael Yates as *Michael*;
Night-watchman Michael Yates as *Mike*.
– One-upmanship *by Stephen Potter*

★

The Manager's Handbook
by Arthur Young

Why use unofficial channels?

- To soften the blow of unpleasant news ('Profits are down; the incentive scheme may not pay out').
- To check reactions to a proposed project.
- To alter or adapt someone else's unwelcome plans, without officially opposing them.
- To add credibility to, or gain acceptance for, official policy.

- To improve your image ('She's actually extremely competent').
- To win advance support for a negotiating position.
- To weaken someone else's bargaining position by stimulating opposition in advance.
- To lift the morale of, say, a team or a department ('We're doing better than expected').
- To lower expectations ('Apparently, we're doing worse than expected').
- To communicate disapproval to subordinates or peers, thus protecting them from the stigma of a more public warning.

★

Understanding Organizations
by Charles Handy

Clearly, if the systems or organizations are to work well, the information must not only be well developed, but it must be well communicated. If there is one general law of communication it is that we never communicate as effectively as we think we do.

★

The other man's word is an opinion,
yours is the truth, and your boss's is law.

COMMUNICATION IN CRISIS

Company Image and Reality
by David Bernstein

1 *Take the initiative.* A company must not try to maintain a low profile. The incident will be subject to speculation in the media long before any official or semi-official

enquiry gets going. Accordingly how a company behaves in the initial period is vital to goodwill – and business.

A company must take the initiative. No news (and 'no comment') will be interpreted as bad news. Silence will imply guilt.

2 *Keep in contact with the media.* Dialogue must start when times are good. This can pre-empt a crisis – or at least mitigate its effect. It will put any bad news in context. It will provide a favourable background for the good news.

3 *Speak the truth.* Journalists are better at detecting lying than company spokespersons are at lying. And anyway telling the truth is always easier.

4 *Treat the media with respect.* The incident is a genuine news item. It probably irks the company to realise it will get more coverage from this than it achieved in total in the past three years. Nevertheless it must realise that the journalist has a job to do and should not assume that he is antagonistic. (Furthermore, relationships forged in fire might well last.) A US company advises its executives:

- The reporter on the scene or on the phone only wants to report the facts, not to pass judgement on our company. The quicker we give him what he needs, the quicker he will move on to another story and permit you to get on with your work.
- Keep a list of news media handy so that you can call them with details if they're not on the scene.
- If you have a camera, shoot pictures.
- As reporters arrive, give them all pertinent information, and advise them regarding photographs.

5 *Do not speculate.* A company must deal in facts. It must assume that everything it says will be quoted. Thus speculation – in the belief that it is 'off the record' – should be avoided.

6 *Do not ask for a retraction.* Misquoting will frequently happen. By then the damage is done. Retraction generally adds to the story's development.

7 *Make sure internal communications are good.* Good internal communications generally indicate good external communications. (This was certainly the case with Johnson & Johnson during the Tylenol crisis.)

8 *Keep your communications simple.* The media don't know as much about the company as the company does. A company should say as much as necessary and no more. A spokesperson should not answer questions that aren't asked. (J&J restricted the discussion to Tylenol, did not discuss other products and guarded the corporate reputation.)

Jargon must be avoided. The journalist a company deals with in a crisis may not be the industry or business journalist the company is usually in touch with. The company can't assume knowledge.

9 *Think of the headline.* This concentrates the mind and condenses the message. The main facts must be communicated first. As with all communication the sender must put himself in the position of the receiver.

10 *Think about the questions.* Similarly, the spokesperson must consider the questions a good, trained journalist will ask – who, what, when, why, where, how? The press release must also answer these questions.

11 *Think in terms of people.* News is about people. Facts, statistics, and stories must be personalised.

12 *Monitor all media coverage.* Only by keeping tabs on every release, every phone conversation, every report, article, comment and news item can the company hope to retain some control of the story. When the media makes a factual error they should report it at once. Communication is continuous dialogue. Keeping tabs teaches the company how media relations works and what works better.

13 *Follow up.* The story isn't over when the crisis ends. The

company should write and thank the media, provide follow-up information, maintain the dialogue.

NEGOTIATING

'The salesman said he'd make me a price if I took them all.'

★

David Bernstein's successful communication company was one of the first to highlight the extent to which communication involved negotiated outcomes. The dynamic nature of modern economies means that negotiations play an increasingly important role in business life. When relationships and roles are fixed and well established the need for negotiation skills is limited. Change and ambiguity force those managers who want to get ahead to develop the kinds of negotiation skills described by Ilich in the piece that follows.

Ancient Roman Advice
Illegitimus non Carborundum
(don't let the bastards grind you down).

★

Deal Breakers and Breakthroughs
by John Ilich

Negotiating guide

- *Exploit your opponents' mental rigidity.*
  Draw out their mental frame with questions.
  Derail their one-track minds.
  Use their predictability to gain an edge.
- *Remain flexible.*
  Prepare for each issue thoroughly.
  Have a general strategy, but avoid a preset formula.
  Expect the unexpected.
- *Identify the person who has final negotiating authority.*
  Don't let them double team you.
  Just ask.
  Don't be fooled by title, age, or appearance.
  Be observant.
  Take few notes.
  Don't let your guard down.
  Watch for the reluctant authority.
- *Reach the final authority through conduits.*
- *Apply the oblique approach.*
- *Assess the authority of the intermediary.*
- *Discover what your opponent fears.*
- *Recognize your own power.*
  Employ the 'power think time' technique.
- *Use your power in a timely manner.*
- *Let your opponent know you have power.*
- *Don't waste your power by holding it in reserve.*
- *Use a variety of sensory stimulations for effective repetition.*

- *Don't lose sight of your primary base.*
  Set specific objectives on each issue.
  Remain cool under pressure.
  Avoid smoking and bad eating habits.
  Take a break when you need one.
- *Identify and use secondary bases.*
- *Don't lose sight of your secondary bases.*
  Avoid distractions.
  Use the list-and-check system.
- *Find new secondary bases during negotiations by asking questions.*
- *Equalize your opponent's every position.*
  Advance positions of equal or greater weight.
  Demonstrate the weakness of your opponent's position.
  Set aside your opponent's position.
  Keep your opponent fully informed about relevant facts.
  Show the irrelevance of your opponent's position.
- *Equalize even far-out positions.*
- *Take advantage of your opponent's failure to equalize.*
- *Always seek to control the negotiations.*
  Try to meet on your home field.
  Try to meet at your best time of day.
  Try to determine the order of discussion.
  Scrutinize the documents your opponents will see.
  Avoid adding new elements.
  Avoid language that will anger your opponent.
- *Practice funnelling.*
  Don't let new elements rewiden the funnel.
  Employ countertactics when needed.
  Make postnegotiation analysis a habit.
  Keep resolved issues closed.
- *Let your opponent make the first offer.*
- *Explain the basis for any offer or counteroffer you make.*
- *Remember: each counteroffer is an entirely new offer.*
- *Use counteroffers to:*
  facilitate the finalizing process, and
  exercise control.

- *Avoid the polarization that comes from unwise ultimatums.*
- *Insert an unless into your ultimatums.*
- *Stay cool when your offer or counteroffer is rejected.*
- *Avoid lowballing and highballing.*
- *Be sure you understand your opponent's offers and counteroffers.*
  Seek clarification if needed.
  Repeat the specifics of the terms and conditions.
- *Respond calmly to lowball or highball offers.*
- *Set deadlines to:*
  create anxiety in your opponent,
  reduce your opponent's options, and
  give yourself greater flexibility.
- *Set deadlines for as short a time as you can justify.*
- *Avoid imposing deadlines on yourself.*
- *Be alert to your opponent's self-imposed deadlines.*
- *Grant deadline extensions only when new facts and/or circumstances warrant.*
- *Seek extensions when your opponent gives you a deadline.*
- *Be persistent in pursuit of your negotiating objectives.*
  Try different approaches.
  Find new arguments.
  Seek new information.
- *Converse with your opponent to find new options.*
- *Remember: persistence is not begging, hassling, harassing, or bullying.*
- *Persistence is an attitude of determination.*
- *Never invite your opponent to 'think the matter over.'*
- *Always ask yourself if your opponent is ready to say 'yes'.*
- *Stay alert for clues that it is time to close.*
  Listen to your opponent's words.
  Pay attention to your opponent's tone of voice.
  Translate your opponent's body language.
  Look for consistency between your opponent's speech, tone, and body language.
- *Question your opponent carefully about negative signs.*

- *Use closing techniques when the time is right.*
  Call upon your opponent to take action.
  Assume your opponent will agree.
  Summarize the substance of the agreement.
- *Don't let your opponent open closed negotiations.*

No one has a better reputation as a negotiator than Mark McCormack. His clients often comment that his special skills as a negotiator have helped them get ahead.

What They Don't Teach You at Harvard Business School
by Mark McCormack

Mean what you say

As a general rule you are far better off having meetings at your own office. This has very little to do with 'power offices' and everything to do with territorial imperative. Even if all you have is a 'power cubicle', it is still best to meet on your own turf.

First of all, it is *your* theatre. You can exercise control over a meeting in your office that you simply don't have elsewhere.

Second, because of the territorial imperative, a meeting on your turf brings with it a sense of 'invasion' by the other party. There is tension there, however, sublimated it may be. Simply by being polite and making the other person feel comfortable you can diffuse that tension, and earn a certain amount of confidence and trust even before the meeting begins.

The only office affectation I allow myself is keeping my lights very low. Otherwise, to me, a 'powerful' office is either a very big one or one that is neat, clean and efficient, a place where one can tell that business gets done.

LOOKING AND LISTENING

McCormack's skills as a negotiator owe much to his early recognition of the difference between negotiation and selling. Injunctions like 'talk less' make sense when you think about it, but many people fail to remember that for a negotiator, talking a lot is not the same as gaining a lot.

What They Don't Teach You at Harvard Business School
by Mark McCormack

Watching people/Reaching people: My seven-step plan

Learning to read people involves a few basic fundamentals:

1 *Listen aggressively*
Listen not only to what someone is saying, but how he is saying it. People tend to tell you a lot more than they mean to. Keep pausing – a slightly uncomfortable silence will make them say even more.

2 *Observe aggressively*
Have you ever said to yourself when watching a chat show or a news interview, 'Oh, that person's nervous,' or 'Aha! That question made him uncomfortable'?

You don't need to read a book on body language to interpret certain motions or gestures, or to 'hear' the statement someone may be making simply by the way he or she is dressed.

3 *Talk less*
You will automatically learn more, hear more, see more – and make fewer blunders. Everyone can talk less and almost everyone *should* be talking less.

Ask questions, and then don't begin to answer them yourself.

4 *Take a second look at first impressions*
I usually go with my first impressions, but only after I've carefully scrutinized them. Some sort of 'thinking out' or contemplative process has to take place between your initial impression and your acceptance of it as a tenet of a relationship.

5 *Take time to use what you've learned*
If you're about to make a presentation or a phone call, take a moment to think about what you know, and what is the reaction you want. From what you know of the other person, what can you say or do to be most likely to get it?

6 *Be discreet*
Discretion is the better part of reading people. The idea of using what you have learned properly is *not* to tell them how insecure you think they are, or to point out all the things you have perceptively intuited that they may be doing wrong. If you let them know what you know, you will blow any chance of using your own insight effectively.

You don't owe anyone an insight into yourself for every insight you have into him. Remember, you can only use what you've learned if he's learned less about you.

The surest way to let people in on your own security quotient is to tell them all about your accomplishments. Let people learn of your qualities and achievements from someone else.

7 *Be detached*
If you can force yourself to step back from any business situation, particularly one that is heating up, your powers of observation will automatically increase. When the other person gets a little hot under the collar, he or she is going to be more revealing than at almost any other time. If you come back with an equally heated response, you will not only be less observant, you will be revealing just as much about yourself.

I am particularly a missionary for the importance of acting rather than reacting in any business situation.

Acting rather than reacting allows you really to use what you have learned. It allows you to convert perceptions into controls. By reacting, by failing to step back first, you are probably throwing this powerful advantage away.

If you don't react you will never *over*-react. You will be the controller rather than the controlled.

★

Achieving real progress in negotiations is the main aim of successful executives like McCormack. This means not getting bogged down or stalled, and recognizing the nature and character of your 'opponent'.

The Haggler's Handbook
by Leonard Koren & Peter Goodman

- *Don't be put off by the word 'no'.* The word 'no' in a negotiation is usually code for 'not right now' or 'not exactly' or 'maybe, but I'm not going to give in just now.' Take similar negative absolutes – like 'impossible', 'never', 'no way' – as invitations to keep talking. After all, if your opponent really thought a deal was out of the question he would get up and leave the room.

  Gambit: When you meet a stone wall of negativity, turn the situation around. Ask your opponent directly, 'What would it take to get you to say yes?'

- *Skip over the points that are bogging you down and come back to them later.* You may find yourself and your opponent thrashing around a certain point without reaching any agreement, or even coming close. Rather than jeopardize the entire negotiation, suggest that the sticking point be put aside for now and returned to after other matters have been settled. By looking at other parts of the negotiation, you may discover a way through the impasse. Also, if you and your opponent can find yourself working together harmoniously elsewhere, you may find it easier to carry that same spirit over to the point of real contention. Whatever you do, don't take trouble at one point as an indication that the entire negotiation is doomed.

- *Unless you have a good reason to trust your opponent, don't.* Be cautious at all times. You can be certain that your opponent is not going to tell you anything to his disadvantage ('the car's frame was bent in an accident'), and you should assume that he is probably stretching the truth ('runs like new'). The basic negotiating rule is, if you can't verify it, don't believe it. Ask for documentation. Become an expert yourself, and check your answers against your opponent's. People will try to make you feel bad for impugning their honesty, for wasting their time. Don't be a sucker. Get everything in writing. If you can't check out all the facts, delay the negotiations or get out of them completely.

- *If your opponent tries to use a dirty tactic, bring it out in the open and discuss it.* When you spot a tricky deal or shady manoeuvre, call attention to it. Once the dirty tactic is exposed, it's lost its effectiveness, and you can then use your opponent's lack of good faith against him. Your opponent may retreat, or he may hang tough. What should you do?

1 Don't attack him personally; that only creates defensive aggression.
2 Offer to 'forget' the incident and suggest moving on to more productive talks.
3 Walk out and wait for your opponent to call you, or call back in a few days and ask whether he's now ready to proceed in good faith.

Variation: Don't expose your opponent's tactic at first, but hold it in reserve until you can milk it for maximum benefit ('By the way, what you tried earlier is a bait and switch, and I'll report you if you don't knock another $150 off the price').

Rosabeth Moss Kanter of Harvard Business School shows in the next piece how the core negotiating skills described by writers like Koren and Goodman are now an integral part of a host of other aspects of business life.

The Changemasters
by Rosabeth Moss Kanter

I could identify a number of tactics that innovators used to disarm opponents: *waiting it out* (when the entrepreneur had no tools with which to directly counter the opposition); *wearing them down* (continuing to repeat the same arguments and not giving ground); *appealing to larger principles* (tying the innovation to an unassailable value or person); *inviting them in* (finding a way that opponents could share the 'spoils' of the innovation); *sending emissaries to smooth the way and plead the case* (picking diplomats on the project team to periodically visit critics and present them with information); *displaying support* (asking sponsors for a visible demonstration of backing); *reducing the stakes* (de-escalating the number of losses or changes implied by the innovation); and *warning the critics* (letting them know they would be challenged at an important meeting – with top management, for example).

★

'Then again, I might be willing to consider a smaller starting salary.'

10 Do What You Gotta Do
Efficiency, Quality and Service

Perhaps the most enduring criticism of MBA programmes, and management education in general, is that they fail to draw out the essentially practical nature of business. Management is about the quality of action, not the quality of analysis. Managers get ahead by taking decisions or initiating actions against which their performance can be judged. In Search of Excellence *highlighted this 'bias for action' as one of the dominant characteristics of the successful business. One of the most enduring and popular stories about Richard Branson centres on his apparent willingness to give out boarding passes if the queues seem too long at the check-in for Virgin Atlantic. This contrasts with the tendency elsewhere for managers to walk past a problem and look for someone to blame, rather than solve the problem immediately.*

There is a powerful operational dimension to this approach to success. In manufacturing, it emerged as a determined effort to understand why problems occur rather than merely tackling the latest symptoms. Toyota's famous 'Five Whys' involves teaching production workers to trace the causes of problems back to their roots. These workers are trained to ask 'why' when a problem occurs. This takes analysis beyond the first layer of difficulty to another layer until the true cause is established and a solution identified. Treating the symptoms of a problem seldom produces a long-term benefit or advantage but can be tempting for the manager seeking a quick fix.

'The Quality Revolution' which occurred over the last decade has affected virtually every aspect of business, in almost all sectors of industry and commerce. It has changed the way people work together as much as the logistics and operations of their firms. The 'revolution' is continuing as

new horizons are discovered and novel ways to get ahead through improved quality are identified. It says much about the way business developed in the post-war era that such a simple proposition – set and deliver the highest standard of operation, finish and reliability to your customers – should need to be stated, and, when stated, should have such an impact.

Quality improvement programmes are built on three fundamental tenets. These are: that everyone in the firm accepts that there are no compromises on quality; that everyone accepts that quality improvement is a continuing process; and that everyone has a part to play in improving quality. Companies will typically use a host of different ways to turn these principles into practices which everyone can understand and employ. Zero Defects has emerged as a means of highlighting the value of absolute standards against more traditional approaches. Brian Moore points out that a 99.99 per cent success rate in landing planes at Heathrow Airport would mean one jumbo jet crash a day. No one would see this as acceptable in the physically and technically demanding world of air transport, so why should it be acceptable elsewhere?

Nowhere has 'The Quality Revolution' been more influential than in services. In part, this reflects the way service was often seen as either a bolt-on to something else or an aspect of the business that was hard to control. The intangibles that produce quality of service pose many problems for managers. They must learn to cope with ambiguity. Users are active participants in shaping the service they and others receive. An airline might be able to control the quality of seats, but what can it do about the terrible cab journey that puts the traveller in a foul mood? A software producer is able to design a new productivity aid, but how does it accommodate the user who tries to link it with an old or unusual operating system? No one holds the car manufacturer responsible for the poor driving of others but hotels are expected to deal with complaints about noisy guests.

EFFICIENCY

Hadley's Law
Don't ever confuse motion with progress.

Few books have had a greater impact on the thinking of managers than In Search of Excellence. *Peters and Waterman identified ten characteristics which many of the most successful firms shared. These were: a bias for action; keeping close to their customers; a willingness to give managers automony so that they could act entrepreneurially; a commitment to getting productivity through people; management styles that emphasized a hands-on approach underpinned by clear values; a policy of 'sticking to the knitting' in choosing areas for development; organizational structures that were kept lean and simple; and policies which gave as much autonomy to people as possible but with core values. They placed a bias for action first, because it influences all aspects of the way managers who want to get ahead, in successful firms, view their role.*

In Search of Excellence
by Tom Peters & Robert Waterman

An excellent company attribute seems to underpin the rest: action orientation, a bias for getting things done. . . .

It's very difficult to be articulate about an action bias, but it's very important to try, because it is a complex world. Most of the institutions that we spend time with are ensnared in massive reports that have been massaged by various staffs and sometimes, quite literally, hundreds of staffers. All the life is pressed out of the ideas; only an iota of personal accountability remains. Big companies seem to foster huge laboratory operations that produce papers and patents by the ton, but rarely new products. These companies are besieged by vast interlocking sets of committees and task forces that drive out creativity and block action. Work is governed by an absence of realism, spawned by staffs of people who haven't made or sold, tried, tasted, or sometimes even seen the product, but instead have learned about it from reading dry reports produced by other staffers.

However, life in most of the excellent companies is dramatically different. Yes, they too have task forces, for example. But one is more apt to see a swarm of task forces that last five days, have a few members, and result in line operators doing something differently rather than the thirty-five-person task force that lasts eighteen months and produces a 500-page report.

The problem . . . is the all-too-reasonable and rational response to complexity in big companies: coordinate things, study them, form committees, ask for more data (or new information systems). Indeed, when the world is complex, as it is in big companies, a complex system often does seem in order. But this process is usually greatly overdone. Complexity causes the lethargy and inertia that make too many companies unresponsive.

The important lesson from the excellent companies is that life doesn't have to be that way. The excellent companies seem to abound in distinctly individual techniques that counter the normal tendency toward conformity and inertia. Their mechanism comprises a wide range of action devices, especially in the area of management systems, organizational fluidity, and experiments – devices that simplify their systems and foster a restless organizational stance by clarifying which numbers really count or arbitrarily limiting the length of the goal list.

★

Change provides a special dilemma for those managers with a bias for action. There is a temptation to avoid action until the final outcome is clear. Rosabeth Moss Kanter highlights the crucial role of 'corporate entrepreneurs' who are willing to accept the risks of change and are capable of managing changes, and who wed their bias for action to the skills needed to implement change. The best of these managers know that their route to getting ahead demands that they continually add value to their firm.

★

The Changemasters
by Rosabeth Moss Kanter

'Corporate entrepreneurs' are the people who test limits and create new possibilities for organizational action by pushing and directing the innovation process. They may exercise their power skills in a number of realms – not only those which are defined as 'responsible for innovation', like product development or design engineering.

I have found corporate entrepreneurs in every function, bringing about a variety of changes appropriate for their own territories. Some were *system builders* (e.g., designers of new market-research departments in insurance companies, of long-range financial-planning and budgeting systems in rapidly growing computer firms). Others were *loss cutters* (e.g., prime movers behind getting foundering products into production faster, behind replacing obsolete quality-control systems in record time). Still others were *socially conscious pioneers* (e.g., developers of task forces to reduce the turnover of women in sales, of new structures to engage employees in solving productivity problems). And there were *sensitive readers of cues about the need for strategy shifts* (e.g., fighters for reduced manufacturing of favoured products because of anticipated market decline, for culling out the losers among 1,200 product options offered to customers).

These 'new entrepreneurs' do not start businesses; they improve them. They push the creation of new products, lead the development of new production technology, or experiment with new, more humanly responsive work practices.

★

Stovall's Law of Negative Inaction
**The only thing wrong with doing nothing
is that you never know when you're finished.**

Heller's approach to adding value leans heavily on the successes achieved by Japanese corporations over the last thirty years. Japanese success in the car industry prompted the Massachusetts Institute of Technology to set up a massive $5m research programme to examine the way companies like Toyota, Honda, Nissan and others achieved this success. Womack, Jones and Roos published the results of their study in The Machine That Changed the World. *The 'lean production' approach of Toyota with its fully involved, highly motivated workforce achieved levels of production and quality standards which were far higher than their US rivals at Framlingham.*

The Pocket Manager
by Robert Heller

Added value. A shiny new concept which is actually as old as the hills. The value added is simply the difference between (a) the cost of all materials and services bought in from outside the firm and (b) the revenue earned from outsiders by the goods and services sold. Why has this simple formula received any attention? What can it add to the familiar notions of profit, contribution, and loss?

One answer is that profit is a residual: what's left after

everything else (except dividends) has been deducted. What it's deducted from, though, is nothing less than added value. That simple difference between (a) and (b) is the pool from which shareholders draw their dividends, lenders their interest – and workers their wages. It also finances the firm's investment in the future, without which it won't have one. It thus follows that if the value added is too low, or if anybody going to the well takes out too much water, somebody or something is going to suffer.

But the reason why the Japanese use the phrase 'added value' so much is different again. They aim for products where they can 'add the greatest value' – meaning those which, because of their market appeal and technological content, achieve the highest mark-up over the bought-in costs. They shun like the plague products where, because of the market situation or the production process, little or no value can be added. The analysis is fundamentally important, not just to profitability (however you calculate it), but to the strength of the company's stance in the marketplace. Value is added by brains rather than brawn – and the brainiest companies never take their eyes off that simple, vital AV statistic.

★

The Machine That Changed the World
by J. P. Womack, P. T. Jones & D. Roos

Our next stop was the Toyota assembly plant at Takaoka in Toyota City. Like Framingham [General Motors plant built in 1948], this is a middle-aged facility (from 1966). It had a much larger number of welding and painting robots in 1986 but was hardly a high tech facility of the sort General Motors was then building for its new GM 10 models, in which computer-guided carriers replaced the final assembly line.

The differences between Takaoka and Framingham are striking to anyone who understands the logic of lean production. For a start, hardly anyone was in the aisles. The armies of indirect workers so visible at GM were missing, and practically every worker in sight was actually adding value to the car. This fact was even more apparent because Takaoka's aisles are so narrow.

Toyota's philosophy about the amount of plant space needed for a given production volume is just the opposite of GM's at Framingham: Toyota believes in having as little space as possible so that face-to-face communication among workers is easier, and there is no room to store inventories. GM, by contrast, has believed that extra space is necessary to work on vehicles needing repairs and to store the large inventories needed to ensure smooth production.

The final assembly line revealed further differences. Less than an hour's worth of inventory was next to each worker at Takaoka. The parts went on more smoothly and the worker tasks were better balanced, so that every worker worked at about the same pace. When a worker found a defective part, he – there are no women working in Toyota plants in Japan – carefully tagged it and sent it to the quality-control area in order to obtain a replacement part. Once in quality control, employees subjected the part to what Toyota calls 'the Five Whys' in which the reason for the defect is traced back to its ultimate cause so that it will not recur.

As we noted, each worker along the line can pull a cord just above the work station to stop the line if any problem is found; at GM only senior managers can stop the line for any reason other than safety – but it stops frequently due to problems with machinery or materials delivery. At Takaoka, every worker can stop the line but the line is almost never stopped, because problems are solved in advance and the same problem never occurs twice. Clearly, paying relentless attention to preventing defects has removed most of the reasons for the line to stop.

At the end of the line, the difference between lean and mass production was even more striking. At Takaoka, we observed almost no rework area at all. Almost every car was driven directly from the line to the boat or the trucks taking cars to the buyer.

On the way back through the plant, we observed yet other

differences between this plant and Framingham. There were practically no buffers between the welding shop and paint booth and between paint and final assembly. And there were no parts warehouses at all. Instead parts were delivered directly to the line at hourly intervals from the supplier plants where they had just been made. (Indeed, our initial plant survey form asked how many days of inventory were in the plant. A Toyota manager politely asked whether there was an error in translation. Surely we meant *minutes* of inventory.)

A final and striking difference with Framingham was the morale of the work force. The work pace was clearly harder at Takaoka, and yet there was a sense of purposefulness, not simply of workers going through the motions with their minds elsewhere under the watchful eye of the foreman. No doubt this was in considerable part due to the fact that all of the Takaoka workers were lifetime employees of Toyota, with fully secure jobs in return for a full commitment to their work.

The basic building blocks of the Japanese approach are described in detail by Professor Chris Voss of London Business School. He draws out the way concepts like Just in Time management are part of a total system of management control.

Just in Time Manufacture
by Christopher A. Voss

Just-in-time management is not one technique or even a set of techniques for manufacturing, but is an overall approach or philosophy which embraces both old and new techniques.

JIT is an approach that ensures that the right quantities are purchased and made at the right time and quality, and that there is no waste.

Benefits of JIT

JIT is characterized by its ability to realize a wide range of benefits, often very rapidly. The short-term pay-offs often far exceed those realized by investments in sophisticated manufacturing technology. (JIT should not be considered a substitute for new manufacturing technology, but in many cases it is a very effective precursor.)

Manufacturing techniques

These are the techniques with which most companies will probably begin their JIT effort. JIT focuses on flow through the operation and cellular manufacturing is one of the core techniques that leads to flow. A key analytical technique leading to cellular manufacturing is group technology. These are supported by set-up time reduction, a key technique that enables manufacture to be in very small batch sizes. Small batch sizes in turn make continuous flow easier to attain. Once these have been implemented, the next technique that can be used is pull scheduling. This is normally known as Kanban, named after the Japanese for the cards that are often used in this system. There are two forms of Kanban, one-card and two-card. These core techniques are supported by a host of other non-core JIT techniques. They include the use of the smallest possible machine, the principles of 'Seiri' (putting away everything that is not needed), 'Seiton' (arranging those things in the best possible way), preventive maintenance, 'Pokayoke' (foolproof devices to prevent mistakes and defects), 'Nagara' (self-developed machines), 'Jidoka' (automatic stopping of the production equipment, automatically or by the worker, when abnormal conditions are sensed or occur), U-shaped lines (within a cell), and standardized packaging and containers.

Implementing JIT

The prime objective of JIT is the elimination of waste. Implementation focuses on making this happen. To implement JIT effectively three areas must be considered. The first is that of quality. Very high levels of quality are a necessary condition for JIT. Any JIT effort must have an accompanying quality improvement programme. One core JIT philosophy is that of continual improvement ('Kaizen'); extra improvement should always be sought. There is no best, only better. This goes hand-in-hand with the technique of enforced problem solving. . . .

Implementation of JIT is also concerned with the most important asset – people. JIT implementation programmes pay particular attention to the involvement of people through such techniques as pushing decision making back down to the cell level, use of multi-functional workforce and small group improvement activities.

★

Thurber's Law
There is no safety in numbers, or anything else.

QUALITY

One of the recurrent themes of The Machine That Changed the World *is the ability of Japanese firms to link volume production and low costs with high quality standards. Chris Voss's earlier piece highlighted the importance of Kaizen – continuous improvement – to improved quality. This is a concept which Philip Crosby has advocated for decades. He sees continuous improvement as a process with a single unifying goal – to produce Zero Defects.*

Quality Without Tears
by Philip B. Crosby

. . . the determination to get things done right just isn't there. I have listened for years as otherwise reasonable people explained and explained how Zero Defects was an impossible goal. Yet, in their own companies, there were areas that routinely had no defects.

Check the payroll department and see how often an error

pops up. Whenever a problem comes about in someone's pay, it is usually because the individual, the supervisor, or the personnel department did something.

Payroll doesn't make mistakes.

Is that because they are such dedicated souls? Certainly they are, but the importance of the work does not necessarily raise performance standards. If that were so, one would think that people working on space exploration equipment never err. However, you can get used to anything, and bad performance standards occur eventually.

The reason payroll does so well is that people just won't put up with errors there. They take it very personally when something is wrong with their paycheck. Not because they think the company is going to cheat them – they know it will all get straightened out eventually. They get upset because they feel that the company doesn't care about them if it can't even get their pay right.

Conventional wisdom says that error is inevitable. As long as the performance standard requires it, then this self-fulfilling prophecy will come true.

The performance standard must be Zero Defects, not 'That's close enough.'

★

Quality Without Tears
by *Philip B. Crosby*

Companies don't do well with quality because they are just not determined enough. I realize this statement sounds as profound as, 'It is better to be rich and healthy than poor and sick.' However, it is true.

[Elsewhere] we discussed the profile of a company that always had problems with quality. Nothing changes until a company breaks that lock.

Quality improvement also has a profile. The companies that don't get much improvement, even though they appear to be determined, have common characteristics:

1 *The effort is called a programme rather than a process.*
   This reflects the idea management holds in its secret heart
   – that this quality business is one of finding the proper set
   of techniques to apply to the proper people. A
   'programme' lets people know that if they wait and go
   through the motions, it will soon be replaced by
   something else. Governments call everything programmes.
   A 'process' is never finished and requires constant
   attention.
2 *All effort is aimed at the lower level of the organization.* It
   is easy to identify this situation. Just try to find something
   that senior management has to do differently: all the
   schooling is for someone else. The Productivity (with a
   capital P) efforts all are for low levels. Quality circles
   never begin in the boardroom. Statistical quality control is
   not applied in white-collar areas.
3 *The quality control people are cynical.* 'Zero Defects is
   Eastern mechanical thinking.' 'We have to satisfy the
   customer's perception of quality.' 'It just isn't possible for

people to do things right the first time.' 'The economics of quality require errors; you have to consider the trade-offs.' All the above are part of the conventional and cynical wisdom that has kept nonconformance an integral part of business. Fortunately, the swing in the quality control profession is toward the reality contained in the Absolutes of Quality Management.

4 *Training material is created by the training function.* The concepts of quality improvement and the actions required to cause it are very subtle and require a comprehension that comes from experience. However, they sound so simple that people get right into training without realizing that they are actually teaching the ideas that caused the problem in the first place.

5 *Management is impatient for results.* As soon as it learns about the cost of quality, management notifies everyone that it expects an immediate reduction. This results in a lot of short-range actions, like shrinking the quality department.

We have learned that there is a 25 per cent reduction in nonconformance costs in the first year if the process is properly applied. There is usually an increase if it is not properly understood.

Impatience also leads to centralization of the programme. This means that the individual managers lay back and wait for the word to come down. That brings everything to a slowdown since it increases the hassle.

These characteristics, and a few more, show up the poorly run quality improvement process. They occur because the entire event has not been thought out and taken seriously enough.

In establishing its determination, management has decided, perhaps without knowing that it has done so, that everyone else needs to do something different. It is not until management decides to clean up its act that real determination sets in.

Philip Crosby and W. Edwards Deming share a mission to transform quality standards in industry. They see this as wholly compatible – even essential – if other business goals are to be achieved.

The Decision Makers
by Robert Heller

Some gurus is good gurus – and none have come any better than W. Edwards Deming. The grand old man of statistical quality control is a latter-day Johnny Appleseed, who, wherever he passes, plants, instead of orchards, upsurges in quality and major improvement in productivity – and profits.

This isn't only because better quality improves sales (it does), and strengthens prices (it does), nor even because better quality control means fewer rejects and thus higher usable output per man (it does). Deming has preached a further sermon all over the world: he has consequently been revered and followed in Japan since the end of the war, with results that are self-evident in every market from cars to semi-conductors: the winning sermon is that deciding to achieve better quality control, and actually doing so, improves everything else.

Behind the dry science lies a passionate belief in man's ability to improve on the poor and the mediocre, and even on the good. If a company like Ford only goes half-way towards living by the creed contained in Deming's fourteen famous points [*see pages 52–4 for the fourteen points in full*], the keys to this all-round improvement and performance, the consequence is a total transformation in its way of life.

★

Kostreski's Theory
If at first you don't succeed – find someone who knows what he's doing.

SERVICE

'I don't know how you managed it, madam, but you have got through to someone in authority.'

The service sector illustrates both the best and worst in quality. It was conventional wisdom until very recently that service industries could not deliver the consistent levels of quality seen in manufacturing. Perhaps inevitably, service entrepreneurs have confounded this wisdom. Marriott Hotels, Disney Corporation, Florida Power and Light, Federal Express and Virgin Atlantic are now by-words for outstanding quality, delivered consistently.

Tom Peters highlights the importance of the 'service promise' in building customer satisfaction based on high levels of service. Passengers using the Virgin Upper Deck service know that the benchmark is the First Class offered by rival airlines. It is the ability of the service company to deliver against this standard that builds customer loyalty. This means understanding the nature of the service experience on the type of dimensions outlined by Zeithaml, Parasuraman and Berry.

Thriving on Chaos
by Tom Peters

Under-promise, over-deliver

With competition heating up in every market, firms are forced to promise the moon to get an order, especially that first order. Right?

Wrong. With an explosion of competitors, many of them new and without track records, reliability, rather than overly aggressive promises, is the most valuable strategic edge, especially for the mid- to long haul. While getting faster at responding to customers is imperative, living up to commitments has never been worth more.

A survey of banks, summarized by Citytrust marketing vice-president Skip Morse, supports this point. Banks with lower customer ratings tend to respond, for instance, to an early-morning customer query with, 'We'll be back to you by noon,' or 'We'll be back to you.' Then they get back to the customer at, say, 3 p.m. The top-rated banks, such as The Morgan, reply, 'We'll be back to you by close of business today' – and they are – at 4 p.m., for example.

The paradox: those banks which, objectively speaking, perform better – that is, which actually get the job done first – are frequently rated lower by customers than those they have apparently outperformed. Customers turn thumbs down on banks that fail to keep promises (3 p.m. instead of noon) or that are vague ('We'll get back to you'), and unfailingly prefer slightly less aggressive promises if these are honoured. . . .

Some intriguing evidence from the health-care field bears on this issue. Surgical patients who are told, in detail, of the nature of post-operative agony recover as much as one-third faster than those left in the dark.

Suppose a patient is told that she or he will suffer severe shortness of breath for four or five days following surgery. Even if the symptoms persist a bit longer than average, the patient is prepared to deal with it. The uninformed patient panics, believing that the operation was a failure. No amount of post-operative explanation helps ('They're lying – I'm dying'). Even if the uninformed patient's shortness of breath lasts less than the norm, his or her emotional distress frequently sets back overall recovery.

We all seek predictability. In fact, the more uncertain, frightening, and complex the situation (such as today's competitive scene), the more we grasp for predictability. That's why I'm not at all surprised at the bank study or healthcare findings.

And yet, as much as we may relate to such stories of frustrating, unkept promises when we are on the receiving end (patient, individual consumer, commercial purchaser), we tend to underrate this concern when we plan our own firm's strategy.

★

Delivering Quality Service
by V. Zeithaml, A. Parasuraman & L. Berry

Ten dimensions of service quality

Dimension and Definition	Examples of Specific Questions Raised by Customers
TANGIBLES Appearance of physical facilities, equipment, personnel, and communication materials.	• Are the bank's facilities attractive? • Is my stockbroker dressed appropriately? • Is my credit card statement easy to understand? • Do the tools used by the repair person look modern?
RELIABILITY Ability to perform the promised service dependably and accurately.	• When a loan officer says she will call me back in 15 minutes, does she do so?

Dimension and Definition	Examples of Specific Questions Raised by Customers
RELIABILITY – *continued*	• Does the stockbroker follow my exact instructions to buy or sell? • Is my credit card statement free of errors? • Is my washing machine repaired right the first time?
RESPONSIVENESS Willingness to help customers and provide prompt service.	• When there is a problem with my bank statement, does the bank resolve the problem quickly? • Is my stockbroker willing to answer my questions? • Are charges for returned merchandise credited to my account promptly? • Is the repair firm willing to give me a specific time when the repair person will show up?
COMPETENCE Possession of the required skills and knowledge to perform the service.	• Is the bank teller able to process my transactions without fumbling around? • Does my brokerage firm have the research capabilities to accurately track market developments? • When I call my credit card company, is the person at the other end able to answer my questions? • Does the repair person appear to know what he is doing?

Dimension and Definition	Examples of Specific Questions Raised by Customers
COURTESY Politeness, respect, consideration, and friendliness of contact personnel.	• Does the bank teller have a pleasant demeanour? • Does my broker refrain from acting busy or being rude when I ask questions? • Are the telephone operators in the credit card company consistently polite when answering my calls? • Does the repair person take off his muddy shoes before stepping on my carpet?
CREDIBILITY Trustworthiness, believability, honesty of the service provider.	• Does the bank have a good reputation? • Does my broker refrain from pressuring me to buy? • Are the interest rates/fees charged by my credit card company consistent with the services provided? • Does the repair firm guarantee its services?
SECURITY Freedom from danger, risk, or doubt.	• Is it safe for me to use the bank's automatic teller machines? • Does my brokerage firm know where my stock certificate is? • Is my credit card safe from unauthorized use? • Can I be confident that the repair job was done properly?

Dimension and Definition	Examples of Specific Questions Raised by Customers
ACCESS Approachability and ease of contact.	• How easy is it for me to talk to senior bank officials when I have a problem? • Is it easy to get through to my broker over the telephone? • Does the credit card company have a 24-hour, toll-free telephone number? • Is the repair service facility conveniently located?
COMMUNICATION Keeping customers informed in language they can understand and listening to them.	• Can the loan officer explain clearly the various charges related to the mortgage loan? • Does my broker avoid using technical jargon? • When I call my credit card company, are they willing to listen to me? • Does the repair firm call when they are unable to keep a scheduled repair appointment?
UNDERSTANDING THE CUSTOMER Making the effort to know customers and their needs.	• Does someone in my bank recognize me as a regular customer? • Does my broker try to determine what my specific financial objectives are?

187

Dimension and Definition	Examples of Specific Questions Raised by Customers
UNDERSTANDING THE CUSTOMER – *continued*	• Is the credit limit set by my credit card company consistent with what I can afford (i.e., neither too high nor too low)? • Is the repair firm willing to be flexible enough to accommodate *my* schedule?

BREAKTHROUGH SERVICE

Some of the greatest successes in service management have been achieved by setting new standards in service. Chris Hart of Harvard Business School has identified the power of unconditional service gurantees. The simplest example of this was probably the Domino Pizza guarantee for its home delivery service: 'If we don't deliver within thirty minutes – you get it free!'

'The Power of Unconditional Service Guarantees'
by Christopher W. L. Hart

One great potential of a service guarantee is its ability to change an industry's rules of the game by changing the service-delivery process as competitors conceive it.

BBBK and Federal Express both redefined the meaning of service in their industries, performing at levels that other companies have so far been unable to match. (According to the owner of a competing pest-control company, BBBK 'is number one. There is no number two.') By offering breakthrough service, these companies altered the basis of competition in their businesses and put their competitors at a severe disadvantage.

What are the possibilities for replicating their success in other service businesses? Sceptics might claim that BBBK's and Federal Express's success is not widely applicable because they target price-insensitive customers willing to pay for superior service – in short, that these companies are pursuing differentiation strategies.

It is true that BBBK's complex preparation, cleaning, and checkup procedures are much more time consuming than those of typical pest-control operators, that the company spends more on pesticides than competitors do, and that its employees are well compensated. And many restaurants and hotels are willing to pay BBBK's higher prices because to them it's ultimately cheaper: the cost of 'errors' (guests' spotting roaches or ants) is higher than the cost of error prevention.

But, because of the 'quality is free' dictum, breakthrough service does not mean you must become the high-cost producer. Manpower's procedures are not radically more expensive than its competitors'; they're simply better. The company's skills-testing methods and customer-needs diagnoses surely cost less in the long run than a sloppy system. A company that inadequately screens and trains temporary worker recruits, establishes no detailed customer specifications, and fails to check worker performance loses customers.

Manpower spends heavily on ways to reduce errors further, seeing this spending as an investment that will (a) protect its market position; (b) reduce time-consuming service errors; and (c) reinforce the company's values to employees. Here is the 'absolute customer satisfaction' philosophy at work, and whatever cost increase Manpower incurs it makes up in sales volume.

Organizations that figure out how to offer – and deliver – guaranteed, breakthrough service will have tapped into a powerful source of competitive advantage. Doing so is no mean feat, of course, which is precisely why the opportunity to build a competitive advantage exists. Though the task is difficult, it is clearly not impossible, and the service guarantee can play a fundamental role in the process.

★

11 Money, Money, Money
Managing Money

Nothing better distinguishes the effectively managed commercial concern from the poorly managed business or public agency than the way money is managed. Money provides the most effective mechanism for monitoring, measuring and controlling performance. This attention to money need not blind managers to the importance of other stakeholder interest. Effective money management can improve understanding of all aspects of the firm's operations. Despite that, many managers feel uncomfortable emphasising the importance of money to success. Sometimes this reflects a lack of confidence in their ability to understand and manage the financial operations of the firm. Perhaps it is better to leave finances to the resident or bought-in experts.

These attitudes probably explain why the same experts are so well paid and so many of the top jobs in companies go to the 'money men'. Most of the fears about understanding money and company finances are unfounded. Money and the way it works in a business is not complicated. It can become complicated through poor presentation by the same financial experts and through jargon and mystique. Managers who get ahead in this area must learn to 'cut through the crap'. An understanding of numbers is an important aspect of this. The financial performance figures can seem imposing to non-expert managers, especially those who do not like to discuss trends, deviations, averages or errors. The simplest maxim for those is to repeat the old KISS principle – Keep It Simple, Stupid. Good money management is important but no one ever stayed at a hotel, bought a car or did their shopping at a store because of the way a firm kept its accounts. Successful non-financial managers force their financial experts to explain or re-present figures until they can be understood and used to improve performance.

These improvements centre on using money to minimize risk or exploit opportunities. Anyone looking closely at the evolution of Virgin over the last decade soon becomes aware of the attention paid to reducing the downside risk. This takes many forms. It means knowing exactly what is involved before an investment is made. Joint ventures share risks among the partners. Sometimes, the most important skill is knowing how to withdraw gracefully with a minimum of losses. This is a tough discipline, especially as the excitement of investments, innovations and expenditures makes the task of asking 'How do we get out if things go wrong?' seem negative and destructive. The managers who survive soon learn a few basic rules about money. Cannon's Money Management Laws are:

1 *All developments cost twice as much as projected.*
2 *All revenues will take twice as long to produce half the forecast income.*
3 *When anyone says everyone will buy it, they mean they don't know who will buy it.*

Managers who want to get ahead rapidly establish simple and easily implemented money management rules or systems. Sometimes they take the form of check-lists. Is our cash flow OK? How do our stock levels compare with those declared by our rivals in their annual accounts? Are we getting paid on time? Other managers have learned the value of comparisons; are planned numbers and actual numbers wildly adrift? How do our margins compare with those obtained by our rivals? Many managers have developed simple rules of thumb which help them improve financial performance and build a base for future growth. These might include: 'tackle overhead costs first', 'whose activities have to be chopped to get real saving?' or 'if in doubt, get out'. It is much easier for managers who have a system to tackle these problems at their root rather than waiting for auditor's recommendations. There is the popular description of auditors as 'those who stand on the sidelines of the battle, waiting until the end so that they can bury the dead and butcher the wounded.'

★

Money isn't everything: usually it isn't even enough.

LIMITING THE DOWNSIDE

The simplest of all money management rules is highlighted by Richard Branson with his advice to limit the downside on any investment. Getting responsibilities clear, sharing risks and making sure that there is an exit route eliminate some of the greatest financial risks.

'Risk Taking'
by Richard Branson

This is my overriding concern. Perhaps it is because we have been a private company and I have often been extremely short of cash that I have never wanted to put the company on the line. However, in retrospect I think it has also been a very important part of getting a good return from our investments. We limit the downside in a number of ways, some of which can seem to be expensive when looked at coldly.

The first way is through the financing structure of a new investment. We will, typically, set up a new company which will employ all the people involved and on whose performance their future will rest. Now, of course, we very rarely walk away from a subsidiary and let it go bankrupt but nevertheless this practice does help focus the minds of the people involved. In addition, we always attempt to arrange the financing of this company so that, as far as is possible, any borrowings or liabilities are without recourse to Group funds. With the airline, we have the banks lending on the basis of the airline's performance and the value of the aircraft themselves. The Group's only obligation to the banks is to provide leadership and management to the team at the airline. This may seem fairly obvious but I can assure you it is not something we see in other companies.

Another example is the entertainment business. There are significant differences between investing in new bands in the music division and investing in a film. Most people see music, films and entertainment generally as being all highly risky business without really understanding how it is possible to manage the risks involved. We invest very heavily in new artistes but not very heavily in films. The difference is that our commitment to new artistes is limited – usually to an initial advance and the marketing and promotional costs of their first few singles and an album. This might commit us to, say, £300,000. If that first album is a success or meets certain criteria, then we go on to a second album and so on, up to eight or nine albums. So, over a few years, our commitment to an artiste might be £3–4m. However, the risk of losing £3–4m has been limited. In contrast, however, if we invest in a film, although its success is no more or less certain than an artiste on the music side, the situation is different. It is not the practice in the film business to contract with talent for anything more than one film. In other words, if a film is successful we have no rights to the future services of the producer, director or cast. An example I know of is Hugh Hudson who was the director of *Chariots of Fire*. His fee for the film was some £200,000. It was of course an enormously successful film and some months later when the production company wanted to have him direct their next film, they found that they had nothing other than a weak moral hold on him and were facing a likely fee level of over $1m. That sort of thing just does not happen in music; therefore we invest heavily in music, not in films.

The second method of limiting the downside is the obvious one about reducing the scale of the risk through joint ventures. Of course joint ventures often actually increase the *degree* of risk in a venture because it adds another variable – e.g. how can two or more people work together satisfactorily? However, it certainly reduces the *scale* of the risk. A good present example of this is our investment in Music Box. This is pan-European television programming based on the hugely successful MTV network in the United States. The total investment required was way beyond the resources of the Group. However, being convinced that this was a good product in a rapidly expanding market, we found a way of going ahead in partnership with Thorn EMI and Yorkshire Television.

The third point to mention is the need to *'have a way out'* of a high risk venture. Very often you will find that one of the greatest risks in investment is lack of flexibility. You get halfway through a project after a year, you get to the point where the only way forward, even if you are then way above budget, is to invest more money – because at that point the marginal decision always seems to encourage ploughing on. That will always be the case unless you have structured the deal so that there is a way out. Again, our best current example is from the airline. We went into the airline business on the basis that we could get out after a year or two, so (using the 'walk away' rule) we said to Boeing that we were not going ahead unless they gave a commitment to buy back the 747 during the first three years of its life at a fixed price. They agreed, so we were able to embark on the airline business, knowing that the downside was very limited. Equally, on the music side of the company, we typically have the right not to proceed with an artist's contract. On our retail side, we make sure that all of our leases or freeholds are easily realizable so that we are not trapped into lossmaking shops.

★

Forde's Second Law
**You can't win them all,
but you can sure lose them all.**

Richard Branson's 'care and control' approach tempers the excitement that financial deals often produce – especially those involving the vast sums described in the following extract from The Bonfire of the Vanities.

The Bonfire of the Vanities
by Tom Wolfe

Sherman and Rawlie led the bond salesmen, reselling the bonds mainly to insurance companies and trust banks – by telephone. By 2.00 p.m., the roar in the bond trading room, fuelled more by fear than greed, was unearthly. They all shouted and sweated and swore and devoured their electric doughnuts.

By 6.00 p.m. they had sold 40 per cent – $2.4 billion – of the $6 billion at an average price of $99.75062 per $100 worth of bonds, for a profit of not two but four ticks! *Four ticks!* That was a profit of twelve and a half cents per one hundred dollars. *Four ticks!* To the eventual retail buyer of these bonds, whether an individual, a corporation or an institution, this spread was invisible. But – *four ticks!* To Pierce & Pierce it meant a profit of almost $3 million for an afternoon's work. And it wouldn't stop there. The market was holding firm and edging up. Within the next week they might easily make an additional $5 to $10 million on the 3.6 billion bonds remaining. *Four ticks!*

By five o'clock Sherman was soaring on adrenaline. He was part of the pulverizing might of Pierce & Pierce, Masters of the Universe. The audacity of it all was breathtaking. To risk $6 billion in one afternoon to make *two ticks* – six and a quarter cents per one hundred dollars – and then to make four ticks – *four ticks!* – the audacity! Was there any more exciting power on the face of the earth? Let Lopwitz watch all the cricket matches he wants to! Let him play the plastic frog! Master of the Universe – the audacity!

The audacity of it flowed through Sherman's limbs and lymph channels and loins. Pierce & Pierce was the power, and he was wired into the power, and the power hummed and surged in his very innards.

★

> Increase of material comforts, it may generally
> be laid down, does not in any way whatsoever
> conduce to moral growth.
> – *Mahatma Gandhi*

BACK TO BASICS

'It's worse than you think; it goes down to the third floor.'

There is often a temptation for ambitious managers to lose track of the basics of financial management. Richard Clemons' comment to me that 'turnover is vanity; profit, sanity; and cash, reality' is echoed in the tight disciplines proposed by Kelly and Kelly and the understanding of commercial reality explored by Heller.

What They Really Teach You at
the Harvard Business School
by Francis J. Kelly & Heather M. Kelly

In order to know whether one is maximizing the value of a company by making appropriate investment, capital management, and financial decisions, ask the following questions:

1 Are the company's financial objectives and strategies consistent with the overall business objectives and strategy of the company? In particular, do the financial strategies reinforce the company's main strategies for differentiating itself from and staying ahead of its key competitors?

2 Is the company's financial performance adequate to support the people and programmes necessary for the company to obtain its short- and long-term goals?

3 Does the company have a system for analysing investment proposals that takes into consideration both the strategic value and the economic value of the investment in relation to the cost of capital required to fund it?

4 Does the company have the appropriate amount of cash available for ongoing operations? Is it able to meet obligations in a timely manner?

5 Does the company's capital structure approximate an optimal capital structure given the business risks, and the objectives and risk preference of the management and the owners?

6 Do the decisions regarding the company's method of funding reflect an appropriate balance of flexibility, risk, income, control, and timing?

★

The Pocket Manager
by Robert Heller

Pareto's Law. The famous 80–20 rule, set out by a 19th century Italian economist, is basic to better management.

Pareto observed that in any series, a small proportion accounted for a large share of the outcome; hence the law's description: 'the significant few and the insignificant many'. Translating that into business terms, 80 per cent of a firm's profits will come from 20 per cent of its products; and 80 per cent of its sales from 20 per cent of its customers.

Analysing a business in this light shows the management where to concentrate its efforts – and, very possibly, which customers to drop and which product lines to cast into outer darkness. But the usefulness of Pareto's Law doesn't stop there. It also tells you that 80 per cent of the value of your stock will be accounted for by 20 per cent of the items held: that 80 per cent of the costs of an assembly will be accounted for by 20 per cent of the components – and, again, this analysis is an essential guide to action.

Concentrate on tight control of the significant 20 per cent and you will achieve vastly greater savings than from effort wasted on the insignificant 80 per cent. The principle is very important in operating schemes like quality circles: you don't want to waste people's time working on problems whose solutions won't make much contribution to the overall result. On the same argument, management ought to watch its own use of time carefully, to ensure that it is concentrating on the vital, not (as happens ridiculously often) on the trivial.

You'll *always* find, on checking, that a Pareto distribution applies – although managers often find it difficult to accept the truth that so much of their effort is relatively futile. Even pay structures tend to follow the law, with the top and bottom pay determined less by greed at the top than by a mathematical relationship. But there are a couple of warnings needed: first, 80–20 isn't a golden mean – the proportions will vary, though the principle won't; second, you can't go on indefinitely chopping out the insignificant many – otherwise, sooner or later, there won't be anything much left at all. Even in the most perfectly efficient company, with the ideally balanced product portfolio and customer profile, Pareto's Law will still apply. The only difference is that the perfection and the ideal will have come about in part by making use of its invaluable guidance.

Getting It to the Bottom Line
by Richard Sloma

Comparisons, comparisons, comparisons . . .

Meaningful questions can only come from rigorous, relative, pertinent, significant, timely, and quantitative comparisons. The essence of an effective, useful management report is a combination of comparisons and the proper presentation of the results of those comparisons.

Just a few specifics which warrant special attention. First, be sure to always show the 'per cent difference' for all critical comparisons. It would be of even more help if the 'per cent difference' column were sorted in either descending or ascending sequence, depending on the nature of the numerators and denominators (see below). Second, and *this is really important*, be sure your reporting system design includes comparative data for *all* of the objectives identified in the Incentive Compensation Programme. Too often, I have seen situations where the Reporting System and the Incentive Compensation Programme were badly out of sync. The net result was as counterproductive and ineffective as it was predictable!

Forget general ledger account numbers!

At least forget about them as far as using them for sequence control fields. Recall that we're trying to prepare a 'management' report. So, then, look to the 'amount' field or the 'per cent difference' field as the proper, effective sequence control. For instance, an Order Backlog Report is much more useful to management if the customers are listed in descending sequence of amount ordered than if they are listed in customer number or alphabetic sequence.

PROFITABILITY

Ensuring profitability requires clearsightedness and the application of the kind of basic disciplines outlined by Bill Scott and Peter Drucker. The approach might shift if circumstances vary but the value of effective controls and a clearsighted search for profits remains.

Into Profit
by Bill Scott

Success models for loss-making companies

The successful models for moving from loss to profit include most of the following:

- Concentrate on reducing costs rather than on increasing sales. Trying to grow out of trouble carries a high risk and is likely to involve unforeseen increases in the cost structure, especially in marketing costs. Look instead for ways to raise production efficiency, for low-cost improvements in production engineering and for reductions in quality costs.
- Find every affordable means of improving customer benefits, especially in the areas of product quality and delivery performance. This can lead quickly to increases in both sales volume and selling price.
- Concentrate on the core business. If necessary, eliminate upstream component manufacturing and contract to the core production process or final assembly where the real value is added to the product. Minimize the involvement in downstream distribution, especially if there is a high call on working capital to finance inventories.
- Avoid all unnecessary risks. You do not have the financial strength to do so. The greatest risks come from moving into new products, new markets or new technologies.

- Become more selective. Concentrate on niche markets where a higher added value can be obtained. Withdraw from undifferentiated market sectors that are dominated by larger and profitable competitors. Above all, do not diversify.
- Cut out significant expenditure that is related to tomorrow rather than today. You may regret it later, but you may at least still be alive to regret it. If necessary mothball the 'star' products until you have turned the corner.
- Make sure the organization is highly motivated towards that one key objective of getting out of the red. You need above-average management and your routes to the market need to be especially well tuned.
- If the problem is a structural one, cut out the cancer as quickly as possible. Restructuring onto a lower fixed cost base with a lower sales volume of higher margin products is the most certain model for success.

★

Graham's Pronouncement, or The Basic Law of Budgets
You can only spend it once.

★

Into Profit
by Bill Scott

How to lower the break-even point

The ways in which the break-even point can be reduced are:

- Reducing the overhead costs.
- Improving the gross margins. An increase in selling price will improve gross margin. So too will reductions in material costs or direct labour costs.
- Making the product mix richer by increasing the proportion of higher-margin products in the sales mix.

Break-even will be achieved by one of the following actions; or by a combination of them:

- Increasing sales towards break-even point.
- Reducing the break-even point

★

Managing for Results
by Peter Drucker

There are several prerequisites for effective cost control:

1 Concentration must centre on controlling the costs where they are. It takes approximately as much effort to cut 10 per cent off a cost item of $50,000 as it does to cut 10 per cent off a cost item of $5 million. Costs, too, in other words are a social phenomenon, with 90 per cent or so of the costs incurred by 10 per cent or so of the activities.
2 Different costs must be treated differently. Costs vary enormously in their character – as do products.
3 The one truly effective way to cut costs is to cut out an activity altogether. To try to cut back costs is rarely effective. There is little point in trying to do cheaply what should not be done at all.

   Typically, however, the cost-cutting drive starts with a declaration by management that no activity or department is to be abolished. This condemns the whole exercise to futility. It can only result in harming essential activities – and in making sure that the unessential ones will be back at full, original cost level within a few months.
4 Effective control of costs requires that the whole business be looked at – just as all the result areas of a business have to be looked at to gain understanding.

'I always say, no pain, no gain.'

Otherwise, costs will be reduced in one place by simply being pushed somewhere else. This looks like a great victory for cost reduction – until the final results are in a few months later, with total costs as high as ever.

There is, for example, the cost reduction in manufacturing which is achieved by pushing the burden of adjustment on the shipping-room and the warehouse. There is cost reduction of inventory which pushes costs of uncontrolled fluctuation upstream onto manufacturing. There is, typically, a great cost reduction in the price of some purchased material which, however, results in longer, slower and costlier machine work to handle the less than perfect substitute material. These examples, as every manager knows, could be continued almost *ad infinitum*.

5 'Cost' is a term of economics. The cost system that needs to be analysed is therefore the entire *economic* activity which produces economic value.

12 I Heard It On The Grapevine

Getting the Best from Information

Many of the changes in quality, operations and management are highly dependent on computers and information technology. These give managers access to information on the different aspects of the firm's operations in ways which enhance their ability to control and direct resources. The wonders of the technology and the variety of new types of data can blind managers to the primary purpose of the technology and the accompanying information, which is, of course, to help them do their jobs better.

Once this fundamental proposition is accepted many of the basic elements of the design and use of good quality management information systems fall easily into place. The most basic of these is that the information provided must be delivered at the right time, to the right people, in a form they can use. This often creates problems for those managing information systems. After all, they control the wonderful technologies. They understand the systems, operations and protocols. Why should they change merely because a marketing, personnel or distribution manager wants information represented in a different or novel way? Older, traditional Data Processing departments are especially fond of this approach. This is why they are largely being replaced by network-based systems which turn the whole system on its head. The focal point of operations shifts from the central machine to the local user. Management Information Systems take as the starting point the needs of users rather than the capacity of systems.

Operating managers are not immune from the effects of this change. Management structures, the skills needed and the nature of management are being changed by the new technologies and capabilities. Whole tiers of management and supervision will disappear. Sometimes this is because the supervisory or control functions they perform are no longer necessary.

Computers can give more senior management up-to-date information on production lines, distribution and turnover without recourse to first and second level supervisors. The changes, however, go deeper than this. Many traditional, hierarchical management systems existed to perform similar control and supervisory functions. Top-down hierarchies are efficient at this but not effective at adapting to change or capitalizing on different skills and ways of working. These structures are rapidly being replaced by 'hub based' structures where the manager operates at the centre of a network. Information, knowledge and insight move on the basis of need rather than protocol. This type of 'organic' structure is more successful and natural than the old-style mechanistic bureaucracy.

Managers who want to get ahead are adapting to these changes in every aspect of their working life. They are learning new skills. It is hard to imagine managers in the future who are not able to specify their information needs, clearly and in terms which fully exploit the capabilities of new technologies. The same managers will probably have a portfolio of relevant technical skills. They will be adept at using word processors, spreadsheets and other productivity tools. They will understand the limitations of technology as well as its capabilities. In all probability, they will manage through their role in networks, not their position in hierarchies.

NEW WORLDS

Information technology has transformed the skills managers need to get ahead. Shoshana Zuboff uses his work with a host of companies across many industries to argue that the change is deeper than this. This effect extends far beyond those directly involved with information systems and technologies. Robert Townsend recognizes this when he advises line managers to wrest control of information technology from the 'priesthood' who seemed in the early years to be winning control of these 'dumb' but powerful machines.

In the Age of the Smart Machine
by Shoshana Zuboff

What is it, then, that distinguishes information technology from earlier generations of machine technology? As information technology is used to reproduce, extend, and improve upon the process of substituting machines for human agency, it simultaneously accomplishes something quite different. The devices that automate by translating information into action also register data about those automated activities, thus generating new streams of information. For example, computer-based, numerically controlled machine tools or microprocessor-based sensing devices not only apply programmed instructions to equipment but also convert the current state of equipment, product, or process into data. Scanner devices in supermarkets automate the checkout process and simultaneously generate data that can be used for inventory control, warehousing, scheduling of deliveries, and market analysis. The same systems that make it possible to automate office transactions also create a vast overview of an organization's operations, with many levels of data coordinated and accessible for a variety of analytical efforts.

Thus, information technology, even when it is applied to automatically reproduce a finite activity, is not mute. It not only imposes information (in the form of programmed instructions) but also produces information. It both accomplishes tasks and translates them into information. The action of a machine is entirely invested in its object, the product. Information technology, on the other hand, introduces an additional dimension of reflexivity: it makes its contribution to the product, but it also reflects back on its activities and on the system of activities to which it is related. Information technology not only produces action but also produces a voice that symbolically renders events, objects, and processes so that they become visible, knowable, and shareable in a new way.

Viewed from this interior perspective, information technology is characterized by a fundamental duality that has not

yet been fully appreciated. On the one hand, the technology can be applied to automating operations according to a logic that hardly differs from that of the nineteenth-century machine system – replace the human body with a technology that enables the same processes to be performed with more continuity and control. On the other hand, the same technology simultaneously generates information about the underlying productive and administrative processes through which an organization accomplishes its work. It provides a deeper level of transparency to activities that had been either partially or completely opaque. . . . technology supersedes the traditional logic of automation. The word that I have coined to describe this unique capacity is *informate*. Activities, events, and objects are translated into and made visible by information when a technology *informates* as well as *automates*.

The informating power of intelligent technology can be seen in the manufacturing environment when microprocessor-based devices such as robots, programmable logic controllers, or sensors are used to translate the three-dimensional production processes into digitized data. These data are then made available within a two-dimensional space, typically on the screen of a video display terminal or on a computer printout, in the form of electronic symbols, numbers, letters, and graphics. These data constitute a quality of information that did not exist before. The programmable controller not only tells the machine what to do – imposing information that guides operating equipment – but also tells what the machine has done – translating the production process and making it visible.

In the office environment, the combination of on-line transaction systems, information systems, and communications systems creates a vast information presence that now includes data formerly stored in people's heads, in face-to-face conversations, in metal file drawers, and on widely dispersed pieces of paper. The same technology that processes documents more rapidly, and, with less intervention, than a mechanical typewriter or pen and ink can be used to display those documents in a communications network. As more of the underlying transactional and communicative processes of an organization become automated, they too become available as items in a growing organizational data base.

In its capacity as an automating technology, information technology has a vast potential to displace the human presence. Its implications as an informating technology, on the other hand, are not well understood. The distinction between *automate* and *informate* provides one way to understand how this technology represents both continuities and discontinuities with the traditions of industrial history. As long as the technology is treated narrowly in its automating function, it perpetuates the logic of the industrial machine that, over the course of this century, has made it possible to rationalize work while decreasing the dependence on human skills. However, when the technology also informates the processes to which it is applied, it increases the explicit information content of tasks and sets into motion a series of dynamics that will ultimately reconfigure the nature of work and the social relationships that organize productive activity.

★

Charley's Observation
Computers were invented by Murphy.

★

Further Up the Organization
by Robert Townsend

First get it through your head that computers are big, expensive, fast, dumb adding-machine–typewriters. Then realize that most of the computer technicians that you're likely to meet or hire are complicators, not simplifiers. They're trying to make it look tough. Not easy. They're building a mystique, a priesthood, their own mumbo-jumbo ritual to keep you from knowing what they – and you – are doing.

Here are some rules of thumb:

1 At this state of the art, keep decisions on computers at the highest level. Make sure the climate is ruthlessly hard-nosed about the practicality of every system, every program, and every report. 'What are you going to do with that report?' 'What would you do if you didn't have it?' Otherwise your programmers will be writing their doctoral papers on your machines, and your managers will be drowning in ho-hum reports they've been conned into asking for and are ashamed to admit are of no value.

2 Make sure your present report system is reasonably clean and effective before you automate. Otherwise your new computer will just speed up the mess.

3 Rather than build your own EDP staff, hire a small, independent software company to come in, plan your computer system, and then get out. Make sure they plan every detail in advance and let them know you expect them to meet every dollar and time target. Systems are like roads. Very expensive. And no good building them until you know exactly where they're going to wind up.

4 Before you hire a computer specialist, make it a condition that he spend some time in the factory and then sell your shoes to the customers. A month the first year, two weeks a year thereafter. This indignity will separate those who want to use their skills to help your company from those who just want to build their know-how on your payroll.

5 No matter what the experts say, never, never automate a manual function without a long enough period of dual operation. When in doubt, discontinue the automation. And don't stop the manual system until the non-experts in the organization think that automation is working. I've never known a company seriously injured by automating too slowly, but there are some classic cases of companies bankrupted by computerizing prematurely.

Since this was written in 1970, the computer-on-a-chip revolution has put desk-top computers in millions of homes and offices, and made two-finger typists of armies of housewives, executives, kids, and other folks. Notwithstanding this major and remarkable development, the human factors remain the same and I stand by what I said, except for the last sentence: because of the reduction in costs of information-processing and communication, the risk of bankruptcy has now shifted in some cases to those who wait too long to automate.

★

Turnauckas' Observation
To err is human; to really foul things up takes a computer.

The pace of change and the flexibility and accessibility of recent generations of computers have already cut the ground from under the priesthood described by Townsend above. Power in the best information systems now lies firmly in the hands of the users, not the processors.

★

Utz's Law of Computer Programming

1 Any given program, when running, is obsolete.
2 Any given program costs more and takes longer.
3 If a program is useful, it will have to be changed.
4 Any given program will expand to fill all available memory.
5 If a program is useless, it will be documented.
6 The value of a program is proportional to the weight of its output.
7 Program complexity grows until it exceeds the capability of the programmer who must maintain it.
8 Make it possible for programmers to write programs in English, and you will find that programmers cannot write in English.

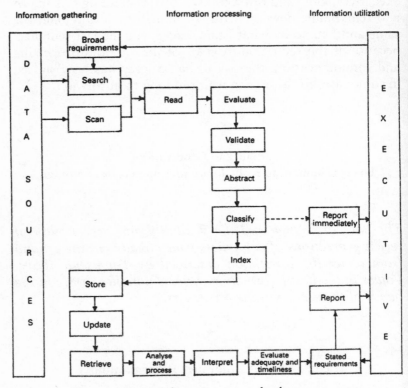

The management information system development process
(*From* Basic Marketing *by Tom Cannon*)

CREATING SYSTEMS

The systems outlined in The Manager's Handbook *are designed to keep power in the hands of information users. This approach calls for managers who understand the capabilities of management information systems and technologies and have the confidence to use their potential to the full.*

The Manager's Handbook
by Arthur Young

It is crucial to ensure that you and other managers understand the business's objectives before establishing the information-processing objectives. Establish an order of priority, ensuring that the system's objectives, if achieved, will satisfy those of the business.

Find out what systems plans exist, and when you have discovered who is responsible for carrying out the plans, determine the best way to communicate with them.

You must clearly establish the role and responsibility which you will assume for your own systems. Where the facilities directly support your business function or performance, knowing the ground rules becomes crucial to your success.

Reviewing a system

- Determine the objectives of the business and the system.
- Order objectives by priority.
- Establish how system performance is measured.
- Identify security procedures.
- Establish responsibility for system operation.
- Establish formal communication between user and provider.

The performance of an automated system
System performance should be examined according to the following two headings:

User satisfaction
Determine the system's level of user satisfaction by finding out:

- How much the system costs to run.
- If the system produces the planned benefits.
- How frequently it has been changed.
- How much changes to the system cost.
- What relationship users have with the computer function.

When you have done that, you should then go on to:

- Review the methods by which computer charges are calculated and passed on to users.
- Find out what support, such as training and advice, has been set up and then make sure that it is followed.
- Ensure that you are kept completely informed of all plans, progress, variances, problems and reasons. Monitor all the various costs and benefits.
- Establish quality control procedures; make sure that your objectives are met.

Checking performance
Examine the reports of the system's performance level. If they do not exist, initiate them on a regular basis and make sure that:

- Reports are, as far as possible, produced on time.
- Users who need to share data are able to do so.
- Terminals are available as planned and response times are adequate.
- Maintenance and break-down procedures are adequate and that they are working as quickly as is necessary.

System management
To manage a system effectively, and be in control of your business area, you should try to:

- Focus on the critical information technology (IT) issues (e.g. response time and what information or level of detail is needed).
- Be aware of the status of all IT matters.
- Increase the awareness of senior management as well as that of your subordinates.

If you can achieve all this, you will be back in the driving seat of your business area. You can then go on to:

- Put into action plans to upgrade your automated systems to meet your demands.
- Address problems in the IT area effectively through the correct channels and methods.
- Test the adequacy of all new applications and procedures supplied by the computer function before you accept them.

Security for the system
Examine the physical and data security procedures for the system:

- Identify threats to hardware, software, data, networks and manpower.
- Ensure adequate documentation is available.
- Take protective measures, e.g. by making certain you are insured.
- Check back-up and security procedures; ensure they are operated.

Draw up a disaster contingency plan by:

- Working out the critical business functions serviced by the computer and plan to be without them.
- Plan and test out recovery procedures.
- Set up a system of regular monitoring to ensure that you are not caught out by any unexpected changes in systems.

★

'Edna, I've brought the boss round for supper.'

★

Weinberg's Law
**If builders built buildings the way the programmers wrote
programs, the first woodpecker that came along
would destroy civilization.**

13 The Times They Are a–Changin'

Managing Change and Innovation –
and Keeping Ahead in the Future

The ability to manage change effectively has always been a mark of the successful managers. In part, this is because managing change is the most difficult and demanding task placed on them. All the systems, values and aspirations of the firm and its members are rooted in the old order. They evolved and persisted because they worked in a specific set of circumstances – one that no longer exists. The incentives or controls that everyone understands and accepts might be wholly unproductive in the new environment. Managing change means managing with at least one hand tied behind your back. This is hard enough but change inevitably means that managers cannot know what will work in the new environment. Will a new incentive system produce the results we need in the new conditions we'll face next year? Honest managers will have to admit they do not know. Managers who want to get ahead because of their skill at managing change soon learn to shift their gaze away from specific solutions to the process of change.

The rate and pace of external change forces managers who want to get ahead to accept that they must innovate to survive and prosper. Successful innovation can reshape the market and the environment to the long-term advantage of the innovator. It involves a set of disciplines which sometimes seem at odds with each other. The ability to think creatively, even to suspend disbelief, stands alongside the need to assess rigorously ideas and proposals. Successful innovations are usually linked with product champions who are skilled and successful advocates of the ideas. The best of these managers are also able to spot when things are going wrong, take remedial action and recognize failure.

★

'I can't seem to remember what used to be there.'

★

Odyssey: From Pepsi to Apple
by John Sculley

The future seems even less predictable today. We have never lived in a time of so much volatile change. It makes planning for the future incredibly complex and difficult, and many companies have lost millions of dollars placing bets on the wrong horses.

OPPOSITION

Anyone struggling to manage change will easily identify with the problems outlined by Machiavelli. It takes a very special kind of manager to accept the responsibility to introduce change. The attacks and brickbats which inevitably follow are enough to discourage even the most determined executives. These and other difficulties go a long way to explaining why no management skills are more prized than those linked with changed management.

The Prince
by Niccolo Machiavelli

And one should bear in mind that there is nothing more difficult to execute, nor more dubious of success, nor more dangerous to administer than to introduce a new order of things; for he who introduces it has all those who profit from the old order as his enemies, and he has only lukewarm allies in all those who might profit from the new. This lukewarmness partly stems from fear of their adversaries who have the law on their side, and partly from scepticism of men, who do not truly believe in new things unless they have actually had personal experience of them. Therefore, it happens that whenever those who are enemies have the chance to attack, they do so enthusiastically, whereas those others defend hesitantly, so that they, together with the prince, are in danger.

New technologies, emerging competitors, shifts in markets and demand are forcing companies to introduce or adapt to change at an ever increasing pace. Companies can no longer hope for periods of consolidation and change but are forced to accept that change is the norm. It is little wonder that the speaker at the General Synod asks 'why cannot the status quo be the way forward?'

The Age of Unreason
by Charles Handy

The scene was the General Synod of the Church of England in the 1980s. The topic being debated was the controversial proposition that women be admitted to the priesthood. A speaker from the floor of the Chamber spoke with passion. 'In this matter,' he cried, 'as in so much else in our great country, why cannot the status quo be the way forward?'

It was the heartfelt plea not only of the traditionalists in that Church but of those in power, anywhere, throughout the ages. If change there has to be let it be more of the same, continuous change. That way, the cynic might observe, nothing changes very much.

Continuous change is comfortable change. The past is then the guide to the future. An American friend, visiting Britain and Europe for the first time wondered, 'Why is it that over here whenever I ask the reason for anything, any institution or ceremony or set of rules, they always give me an historical answer – because . . ., whereas in my country we always want a functional answer – in order to . . .' Europeans, I suggested, look backwards to the best of their history and change as little as they can; Americans look forward and want to change as much as they may.

Circumstances do, however, combine occasionally to discomfort the advocates of the status quo.

The problem with protecting the 'status quo' is that the outside world intrudes. Charles Handy touches on the fate of the Peruvian Indians. He also points out that it is often easier to adapt to dramatic change than to gradual change. The former forces a reaction while a delayed response to the latter may come too late to do any good.

The Age of Unreason
by Charles Handy

I like the story of the Peruvian Indians who, seeing the sails of their Spanish invaders on the horizon put it down to a freak of the weather and went on about their business, having no concept of sailing ships in their limited experience. Assuming continuity, they screened out what did not fit and let disaster in. I like less the story that a frog if put in cold water will not bestir itself if that water is heated up slowly and gradually and will in the end let itself be boiled alive, too comfortable with continuity to realize that continuous change at some point becomes discontinuous and demands a change in behaviour. If we want to avoid the fate of the Peruvian Indians or the boiling frog we must learn to look for and embrace discontinuous change.

That is more revolutionary than it sounds. Discontinuous, after all, is hardly a word to stir the multitudes; yet to embrace discontinuous change means, for instance, completely re-thinking the way in which we learn things.

★

FUTURES

It is impossible to stop or ignore the kinds of change outlined by John Naisbitt and Patricia Aburdene. Firms have no choice but to adapt to the demands of new kinds of workers, consumers and families.

Re-inventing the Corporation
by John Naisbitt & Patricia Aburdene

The profile of today's average worker looks something like this:

- A thirty-four-year-old baby boomer with two children and a working spouse,
- who plans to work past retirement (and expects to because of the insecurities of the Social Security system),
- who does not belong to a union and would not consider joining one,

- who is willing to accept a certain amount of risk in exchange for the possibility of being rewarded for superior performance,
- who is increasingly likely to have some sort of flexible work schedule – or would prefer one.
- Increasingly, that 'average worker' is a woman.

REENGINEERING

The changes described by John Naisbitt and Patricia Aburdene create opportunities for those firms able to reengineer their operations to fit the new environment.

Reengineering the Corporation
by Michael Hammer & James Champy

For two hundred years people have founded and built companies around Adam Smith's brilliant discovery that industrial work should be broken down into its simplest and most basic *tasks*. In the postindustrial business age we are now entering, corporations will be founded and built around the idea of reunifying those tasks into coherent business *processes* . . .

Corporations *can* reinvent themselves. We call the techniques they can use to accomplish this *business reengineering* . . .

Business reengineering means starting all over, starting from scratch.

Business reengineering means putting aside much of the received wisdom of two hundred years of industrial management. It means forgetting how work was done in the age of the mass market and deciding how it can best be done now. In business reengineering, old job titles and old organizational arrangements – departments, divisions, groups, and so on – cease to matter. They are artifacts of another age. What matters in reengineering is how we want to organize work today, given the demands of today's markets and the power of today's technologies. How people and companies did things yesterday doesn't matter to the business reengineer . . .

At the heart of business reengineering lies the notion of *discontinuous thinking* – identifying and abandoning the outdated rules and fundamental assumptions that underlie current business operations. Every company is replete with implicit rules left over from earlier decades: 'Customers don't repair their own equipment.' 'Local warehouses are necessary for good service.' 'Merchandising decisions are made at headquarters.' These rules are based on assumptions about technology, people, and organizational goals that no long hold. Unless companies change these rules, any superficial reorganizations they perform will be no more effective than dusting the furniture in Pompeii.

★

'I should caution you that the position you're applying for involves prolonged periods of boredom, punctuated with episodes of overwhelming chaos.'

THE FEATURES OF CHANGE

Executives who want to get ahead by managing change effectively must understand the processes involved and the way actions and their consequences influence the ability of their company and their colleagues to adapt.

Enterprise
by Tom Cannon

Lewin was among the first writers to suggest that managing change is best viewed as a multi-stage process. He emphasized three basic steps: 'unfreezing,' 'change' and 'refreezing'. Unfreezing involves those activities designed to break down the barriers to change and identify the part people and groups play in easing through the change. Change is 'the movement from an old state to a new one'. Refreezing is the creation of the new *status quo*. This is usually accompanied by some reassurance about the future. . . .

Change agents help with these developments. Their value derives from a mixture of status, trust, expertise, credibility and focus. Status derives from their role as leaders. Trust is important as it provides leeway for the inevitable breakdowns in communication. Expertise provides the change agent with a series of templates applied to situations to minimize costly errors and achieve results with a minimum of effort. Credibility reassures other players that the results will justify the effort. The agent will provide a useful focus for those members of the organization advocating and backing change. Continued support for the developments and those shaping their implementation is necessary from all members of the leadership group. This needs to be shown through deeds and words. Perhaps the easiest way to undermine change is for members of the leadership group to undermine those responsible for change.

McGuinness had been put in charge of several players nearing the ends of their careers who had managerial ambitions of their own. It was easy for them to mutter how they could have done things better. The close contact that some kept with Sir Matt – Denis Law, Pat Crerand and Willie Morgan, for instance – on the golf course or in restaurants on Saturday nights maintained a channel for discontent, perhaps more imagined than real. 'I didn't mind other players going behind my back,' McGuinness said recently. 'What I did mind was that he accepted their side of the story rather than mine.'

(From *Manchester United* by M. Crick and D. Smith.)

Resistance to change occurs at an individual and organizational levels. People oppose because the proposals challenge existing ways of behaving and provoke fears of the unknown. Some threats are real. People recognize they may be unable to adapt and find their position under threat. The innovations challenge their past behaviour and raise questions about its value. These hurdles are reinforced by organizational resistance. Established power and authority systems may be challenged. Change costs money. The proposals may not sit well within the current structure. Success will turn on the manager's ability to overcome these obstacles while retaining organization coherence and prosperity.

Progress is likely where:

- the need for change is recognized and internalized.
- communication and participation are high.
- innovation is endorsed.
- early successes are recognized and disseminated.
- the leadership group acts together.
- change is underpinned with training and development.
- a holistic view of the enterprise is adopted.
- consultation is used for feedback, local ownership and response.

- implementation takes into account the need for staff development and modification.
- all recognize that if anything can go wrong, it will go wrong.

★

Finagle's Rules

Ever since the first scientific experiment, man has been plagued by the increasing antagonism of nature. It seems only right that nature should be logical and neat, but experience has shown that this is not the case. A further series of rules has been formulated, designed to help man accept the pigheadedness of nature:

1 To study a subject best, understand it thoroughly before you start.
2 Always keep a record of data. It indicates you've been working.
3 Always draw your curves, then plot the reading.
4 In case of doubt, make it sound convincing.
5 Experiments should be reproducible. They should all fail in the same way.
6 Do not believe in miracles. Rely on them.
7 If an experiment works, something has gone wrong.
8 No matter what result is anticipated, there will always be someone eager to (a) misinterpret it, (b) fake it, or (c) believe it happened to his own pet theory.
9 In any collection of data, the figure most obviously correct, beyond all need of checking, is the mistake.
   Corollary 1: No one whom you ask for help will see it.
   Corollary 2: Everyone who stops by with unsought advice will see it immediately.
10 Once a job is fouled up, anything done to improve it only makes it worse.
11 Science is truth – don't be misled by facts.

PERSISTENCE

The successful champions of change succeed because they ask the kind of fundamental questions highlighted by Mike Hammer and Jim Champy. These basic questions can produce the type of radical and dramatic shifts that give a powerful competitive edge to companies.

Reengineering the Corporation
by Michael Hammer & James Champy

Reengineering formally defined

This definition contains four key words:

1 *Fundamental*
The first key word is 'fundamental.' In doing reengineering, businesspeople must ask the most basic questions about their companies and how they operate: *Why* do we do what we do? And why do we do it the way we do? Asking these fundamental questions forces people to look at the tacit rules and assumptions that underlie the way they conduct their businesses. Often, these rules turn out to be obsolete, erroneous, or inappropriate.
Reengineering begins with no assumptions and no givens.

2 *Radical*
The second key word in our definition is radical, which is derived from the Latin word 'radix,' meaning root. Radical redesign means getting to the root of things: not making superficial changes or fiddling with what is already in place, but throwing away the old.

3 *Dramatic*
The third key word is *dramatic.* Reengineering isn't about making marginal or incremental improvements but about achieving quantum leaps in performance. If a company falls 10

per cent short of where it should be, if its costs come in 10 per cent too high, if its quality is 10 per cent too low, if its customer service performance needs a 10 per cent boost, that company does *not* need reengineering. More conventional methods, from exhorting the troops to establishing incremental quality programmes, can dig a company out of a 10 per cent hole. Reengineering should be brought in only when a need exists for heavy blasting. Marginal improvement requires fine-tuning; dramatic improvement demands blowing up the old and replacing it with something new.

4 *Processes*
The fourth key word in our definition is *processes*. Although this word is the most important in our definition, it is also the one that gives most corporate managers the greatest difficulty. Most businesspeople are not 'process-oriented'; they are focused on tasks, on jobs, on people, on structures, but not on processes.

We define a business process as a collection of activities that takes one or more kinds of input and creates an output that is of value to the customer. [An example of a process is] order fulfillment, which takes an order as its input and results in the delivery of the ordered goods. In other words, the delivery of the ordered goods to the customer's hands is the value that the process creates.

Firms ambitious enough to reengineer themselves attract some of the most talented people. They will want to use their knowledge and intuition to get ahead.

Re-inventing the Corporation
by John Naisbitt & Patricia Aburdene

1 The best and brightest people will gravitate toward those corporations that foster personal growth.
2 The manager's new role is that of coach, teacher, and mentor.

3 The best people want ownership – psychic and literal – in a company; the best companies are providing it.
4 Companies will increasingly turn to third-party contractors, shifting from hired labour to contract labour.
5 Authoritarian management is yielding to a networking, people style of management.
6 Entrepreneurship within the corporations – intrapreneurship – is creating new products and new markets and revitalizing companies inside out.
7 Quality will be paramount.
8 Intuition and creativity are challenging the 'it's all in the numbers' business-school philosophy.
9 Large corporations are emulating the positive and productive qualities of small business.
10 The dawn of the information economy has fostered a massive shift from infrastructure to quality of life.

★

'When they goof off, they call it networking!'

INNOVATION

Much of the pressure for change comes from the determination of people and firms to innovate and find new ways to tackle issues. Effective innovation is probably the single most important factor in corporate success. Rosabeth Moss Kanter highlights the importance of learning and relearning the lessons of past achievements.

Galileo's Conclusion
Science proceeds more by what it has learned to ignore than by what it takes into account.

★

The Changemasters
by Rosabeth Moss Kanter

The 'Roast Pig' problem

Pervading the time of institutionalizing innovations, when leaders want to ensure that their benefits can be derived repeatedly, is the nagging question of defining accurately the practice or method or cluster of attributes that is desired. Out of all the events and elements making up an innovation, what is the core that needs to be preserved? What *is* the essence of the innovation? This is a problem of theory, an intellectual problem of understanding exactly *why* something works.

I call this the 'Roast Pig' problem after Charles Lamb's classic 1822 essay 'A Dissertation on Roast Pig,' a satirical account of how the art of roasting was discovered in a Chinese village that did not cook its food. A mischievous child accidentally set fire to a house with a pig inside, and the villagers poking around in the embers discovered a new delicacy. This eventually led to a rash of house fires. The moral of the story is: when you do not understand how the pig gets cooked, you have to burn a whole house down every time you want a roast-pork dinner.

The 'Roast Pig' problem can plague any kind of organization that lacks a solid understanding of itself. One striking example comes from a high-technology firm I'll call 'Precision Scientific Corporation.' Precision grew steadily and rapidly from its founding to a position of industry preeminence. To the founders, many of whom still manage it, this success is due to a strongly entrepreneurial environment and an equally strong aversion to formal bureaucratic structures. But recently, growth has slackened, margins are down, competition is up, and Precision is even beginning to contemplate cutting back the work force. Increasingly Precision's leaders have the feeling that something needs to be done, but cannot agree on what it should be.

One obvious issue at Precision is waste and duplication. For example, there are a dozen nearly identical model shops on the same small site, neighbouring operating units have their own systems for labelling and categorizing parts, and purchases tend to be haphazard and uncoordinated. But although this is well known, and although a number of middle-level 'entrepreneurs' surface from time to time with systems innovations to solve the problems, the leaders express considerable reluctance to change anything. So each wave of good ideas for operational improvements that washes up from the middle goes out again with the tide.

The reason is simple: Roast Pig. Precision senior executives have been part of a very successful history, but they do not seem to fully understand that history. They have no theory to guide them. They do not act as though they knew exactly which aspects of the culture and structure they have built are critical, and which could profitably and safely be modified. They are afraid that changing *anything* would begin to unravel *everything*, like a loosely knit sweater. In the absence of a strong theory, they feel compelled to keep burning down the houses, even though house costs are rising and other villages are reputed to have learned new and less expensive cooking methods.

In many companies, management practices are much more

vulnerable to the Roast Pig problem than products, because the depth of understanding of technology and markets sometimes far exceeds the understanding of organizational behaviour and organizational systems. So among a dozen failures to diffuse successful work innovations were a number that did not spread because of uncertainty or confusion about what the 'it' was that was to be used elsewhere. Or I see 'superstitious behaviour,' the mindless repetition of unessential pieces of a new practice in the false belief that it will not work without them – e.g., in the case of quality circles which companies often burden with excessive and unnecessary formulas for their operation from which people become afraid to depart.

★

The Changemasters
by Rosabeth Moss Kanter

Experience after experience with innovations that fizzle after a bright start, be they new participative work systems or new products, shows that external relations are a critical factor: the connections, or lack of them, between the area initially producing the innovation and its neighbourhood and beyond. It appears that workplace innovations do best at the extremes: when they occur in units with total autonomy, so that the area is much less vulnerable to the surrounding environment; or when the innovating units are well integrated with the larger units in which they are nested. The problems come about when there is dependence but not integration.

★

NEW PRODUCT DEVELOPMENT

Innovation is closely linked with new product and service development. In part, this is because of the constant pressure for novel ideas and products. Ted Levitt's classic article on the

Product Life Cycle shows how this pressure shapes the way markets evolve over time. In effect, it means that managers must be planning to replace their most successful products even before they are mature.

'Exploiting the Product Life Cycle'
by T. Levitt

For companies interested in continued growth and profits, successful new product strategy should be viewed as a planned totality that looks ahead over some years. For its own good, new product strategy should try to predict in some measure the likelihood, character, and timing of competitive and market events. While prediction is always hazardous and seldom very accurate, it is undoubtedly far better than not trying to predict at all. In fact, every product strategy and every business decision inescapably involves making a prediction about the future, about the market, and about competitors. To be more systematically aware of the predictions one is making so that one acts on them in an offensive rather than a defensive or reactive fashion – this is the real virtue of preplanning for market stretching and product life extension. The result will be a product strategy that includes some sort of *plan for a timed sequence of conditional moves.*

Even before entering the market development stage, the

originator should make a judgment regarding the probable length of the product's normal life, taking into account the possibilities of expanding its uses and users. This judgment will also help determine many things – for example, whether to price the product on a skimming or a penetration basis, or what kind of relationship the company should develop with its resellers.

These considerations are important because at each stage in a product's life cycle each management decision must consider the competitive requirements of the next stage. Thus a decision to establish a strong branding policy during the market growth stage might help to insulate the brand against strong price competition later; a decision to establish a policy of 'protected' dealers in the market development stage might facilitate point-of-sale promotions during the market growth state, and so on. In short, having a clear idea of future product development possibilities and market development opportunities should reduce the likelihood of becoming locked into forms of merchandising that might possibly prove undesirable. . . .

To illustrate the virtue of pre-introduction planning for a product's later life, suppose a company has developed a non-patentable new product – say, an ordinary kitchen salt shaker. Suppose that nobody now has any kind of shaker. One might say, before launching it, that (1) it has a potential market of 'x' million household, institutional, and commercial consumers, (2) in two years market maturity will set in, and (3) in one year profit margins will fall because of the entry of competition. Hence one might lay out the following plan:

1 *End of first year: expand market among current users.*
   Ideas – new designs, such as sterling shaker for formal use, 'masculine' shaker for barbecue use, antique shaker for 'Early American' households, miniature shaker for each table place setting, moisture-proof design for beach picnics.
2 *End of second year: expand market to new users.*
   Ideas – designs for children, quaffer design for beer

drinkers in bars, design for sadists to rub salt into open wounds.
3 *End of third year: find new uses.*
Ideas – make identical product for use as a pepper shaker, as decorative garlic salt shaker, shaker for household scouring powder, shaker to sprinkle silicon dust on parts being machined in machine shops, and so forth.

This effort to prethink methods of reactivating a flattening sales curve far in advance of its becoming flat enables product planners to assign priorities to each task, and to plan future production expansion and capital and marketing requirements in a systematic fashion. It prevents one's trying to do too many things at once, results in priorities being determined rationally instead of as accidental consequences of the timing of new ideas, and disciplines both the product development effort that is launched in support of a product's growth and the marketing efforts that is required for its continued success.

Sometimes the problems of managing change, innovating and building successful new products seem so great that it's easy to forget the accomplishments of those managers and firms who get ahead in these areas. Tom Peters gives an invaluable checklist (despite Americanisms like 'at-bats') while Rosabeth Moss Kanter adds perspective to the issues.

Liberation Management
by Tom Peters

The pursuit of luck

Innovation is a low-odds business – and luck sure helps. (It's jolly well helped me!) If you believe that success does owe a lot to luck, and that luck in turn owes a lot to getting in the way of unexpected opportunities, you need not throw up your hands in despair. There *are* strategies you can pursue to get a little nuttiness into your life, and perhaps, then, egg on good luck.

(By contrast, if you believe that orderly plans and getting up an hour earlier are the answer, then by all means arise before the rooster and start planning.)

Want to get lucky? Try following these 50(!) strategies:

1 At-bats. More times at the plate, more hits.
2 Try it. Cut the baloney and get on with *something*.
3 Ready. Fire. Aim. (Instead of Ready. Aim. Aim. Aim. . . .)
4 'If a thing is worth doing, it is worth doing badly.' – G. K. Chesterton. You've gotta start somewhere.
5 Read odd stuff. Look anywhere for ideas.
6 Visit odd places. Want to 'see' speed? Visit CNN.
7 Make odd friends.
8 Hire odd people. Boring folks, boring ideas.
9 Cultivate odd hobbies. Raise orchids. Race yaks.
10 Work with odd partners.
11 Ask dumb questions. 'How come computer commands all come from keyboards?' *Somebody* asked that one first; hence, the mouse.
12 Empower. The more folks feel they're running their own show, the more at-bats, etc.
13 Train without limits. Pick up the tab for training unrelated to work – keep everyone engaged, period.
14 Don't back away from passion. 'Dispassionate innovator' is an oxymoron.
15 Pursue failure. Failure is success's only launching pad. (The bigger the goof, the better!)
16 Take anti-NIH pills. Don't let 'not invented here' keep you from ripping off nifty ideas.
17 Constantly reorganize. Mix, match, try different combinations to shake things up.
18 Listen to everyone. Ideas come from anywhere.
19 Don't listen to anyone. Trust your inner ear.
20 Get fired. If you're not pushing hard enough to get fired, you're not pushing hard enough. (More than once is OK.)

21 Nurture intuition. If you can find an interesting market idea that came from a rational plan, I'll eat *all* my hats. (I have a collection.)

22 Don't hang out with 'all the rest'. Forget the same tired trade association meetings, talking with the same tired people about the same tired things.

23 Decentralize. At-bats are proportional to the amount of decentralization.

24 Decentralize again.

25 Smash all functional barriers. Unfettered contact among people from different disciplines is magic.

26 Destroy hierarchies.

27 Open the books. Make everyone a 'businessperson', with access to all the financials.

28 Start an information deluge. The more real-time, unedited information people close to the action have, the more that 'neat stuff' happens.

29 Take sabbaticals.

30 'Repot' yourself every ten years. (This was the advice of former Stanford Business School dean Arjay Miller – meaning change careers each decade.)

31 Spend 50 per cent of your time with 'outsiders.' Distributors and vendors will give you more ideas in five minutes than another five-hour committee meeting.

32 Spend 50 per cent of your 'outsider time' with wacko outsiders.

33 Pursue alternative rhythms. Spend a year on a farm, six months working in a factory or burger shop.

34 Spread confusion in your wake. Keep people off balance, don't let the ruts get deeper than they already are.

35 *Dis*organize. Bureaucracy takes care of itself. The boss should be 'chief dis-organizer,' Quad/Graphics CEO Harry Quadracci told us.

36 'Dis-equilibrate. . . . Create instability, even chaos.' Good advice to 'real leaders' from Professor Warren Bennis.

37 Stir curiosity. Igniting youthful, dormant curiosity in

followers is the lead dog's top task, according to Sony chairman Akio Morita.

38 Start a Corporate Traitors' Hall of Fame. 'Renegades' are not enough. You need people who despise what you stand for.

39 Give out 'Culture Scud Awards'. Your best friend is the person who attacks your corporate culture head-on. Wish her well.

40 Vary your pattern. Eat a different breakfast cereal. Take a different route to work.

41 Take off your coat.

42 Take off your tie.

43 Roll up your sleeves.

44 Take off your shoes.

45 Get out of your office. Tell me, honestly, the last time something inspiring or clever happened at that big table in your office?!

46 Get rid of your office.

47 Spend a workday each week at home.

48 Nurture peripheral vision. The interesting 'stuff' usually is going on beyond the margins of the professional's ever-narrowing line of sight.

49 Don't 'help'. Let the people who work for you slip, trip, fall – and grow and learn on their own.

50 Avoid moderation in all things. 'Anything worth doing is worth doing to excess,' according to Edwin Land, Polaroid's founder.

Now write down the opposite of each of the 50. Which set comes closer to your profile?

In short, loosen up!

★

When Giants Learn to Dance
by Rosabeth Moss Kanter

The new game brings with it new challenges. The mad rush to improve performance and to pursue excellence has multiplied the number of demands on executives and managers. These demands come from every part of business and personal life, and they increasingly seem incompatible and impossible:

- Think strategically and invest in the future – but keep the numbers up today.
- Be entrepreneurial and take risks – but don't cost the business anything by failing.
- Continue to do everything you're currently doing even better – and spend more time communicating with employees, serving on teams, and launching new projects.
- Know every detail of your business – but delegate more responsibility to others.
- Become passionately dedicated to 'visions' and fanatically committed to carrying them out – but be flexible, responsive, and able to change direction quickly.
- Speak up, be a leader, set the direction – but be participative, listen well, cooperate.
- Throw yourself wholeheartedly into the entrepreneurial game and the long hours it takes – and stay fit.
- Succeed, succeed, succeed – and raise terrific children.

★

The best laid plans of mice and men are usually about equal.

14 I Will Survive

Learning from Mistakes and Coping with Adversity

Failure plays a surprisingly prominent part in many business success stories. Henry Ford, it is said, only developed the Model T because the tractors he built were failures. Edison's 'ticker tape' machine worked, but his failure to secure the patents 'forced' him to look for new areas for work – like developing electric lighting. It is surprisingly hard to find successful managers who got it right first time. The willingness to get up after getting knocked down and to learn from failure is perhaps the single most enduring feature of greatness in managers. It is this mixture of determination to succeed allied to the ability to learn the lessons of failure which recurs in the history of success.

★

Jones' Law
The man who can smile when things go wrong
has thought of someone he can blame it on.

LEARNING FROM MISTAKES

Getting ahead means taking risks. Sometimes these risks lead to failures. Charles Handy points out how successful firms have learned to absorb and learn from failure. It is a view which gains sympathy from Richard Branson who spent time looking at the problems faced by Laker before he launched Virgin Atlantic.

The Age of Unreason
by Charles Handy

The missing forgiveness

I asked an American the secret of his firm's obviously successful development policy. He looked me straight in the eye. 'Forgiveness,' he said. 'We give them big jobs and big responsibilities. Inevitably they make mistakes, we can't check them all the time and don't want to. They learn, we forgive, they don't make the mistake again.'

He was unusual. Too many organizations use their appraisal schemes and their confidential files to record our errors and our small disasters. They use them to chastise us with, hoping to inspire us, or to frighten us to do better. It might work once but in future we will make sure that we do not venture far enough from the beaten track to make any mistake. Yet no experiment, no test of new ideas, means no learning and no change. As in organizations, so it can be in families.

The evidence is quite consistent, if you reward the good and ignore or forgive the bad, the good will occur more frequently and the bad will gradually disappear. A concern over trouble in the classroom led to research into the way teachers allocated praise and blame. About equally, it seemed, except that all praise was for academic work and all blame was for behaviour. The teachers were coached to *only* give praise, for both academic work and good behaviour and to *ignore* the bad. It worked. Within a few weeks unruly behaviour had almost disappeared.

More difficult than forgiving others is to forgive oneself. That turns out to be one of the real blocks to change. We as individuals need to accept our past but then to turn our backs on it. Organizations often do it by changing their name, individuals by moving house, or changing spouses. It does not have to be so dramatic. Scrapbooks, I believe, are useful therapy – they are a way of putting the past to bed, decorously. Then we can move forward.

★

Nolan's Observation
**The difference between smart people and dumb people
isn't that smart people don't make mistakes. They just
don't keep making the same mistake
over and over again.**

★

From a paper on 'Entrepreneurship'
by Richard Branson

If there's one thing above all from which I've learnt how to survive in busines, it's been from making mistakes – and the more mistakes you make the more you learn. Not that I'm suggesting failures are ever welcome at the time. The key point is not to let them get you down, to accept them, and then to make sure never to make the same mistakes again.

But your own mistakes are not the only ones you can learn from. It can also be very helpful to analyse the mistakes of others. This was especially so in the decision to set up an airline, in 1984.

The Laker collapse was still fresh in people's minds – and was no doubt what made people think I was out of my mind. Laker was a transatlantic airline whose marketing principle was based only on price competition with the major carriers. What people didn't know was that I'd paid close attention to the mistakes which appeared to have caused the failure, as well as what might be done to avoid repeating them.

For example, we would obviously need to protect ourselves against currency fluctuations. We should go for carrying freight as well as passengers, and that would mean using 747s instead of DC10s. By concentrating too exclusively on offering a discount price led service, Laker had made themselves very vulnerable to price cutting by the bigger carriers. And by the time they introduced a business class – two months before the collapse – it was too late.

So we decided to have a unique and high quality business class right from the start, to complement a competitive and good economy class. It wasn't just that it had the potential to pay for lower fares in economy class – which in fact is what has happened. It also meant we'd have a regular clientele who wouldn't desert us at the first hint of a skirmish in the price war.

Seven years later, lessons learnt from the misfortunes of others have paid off. Upper Class, Virgin Atlantic's business class, has won a string of awards from the travel press. And it's so heavily booked on some routes that it's expanded way beyond the upstairs cabin to occupy half the space on the plane.

★

**Those who cannot remember the past
are condemned to repeat it.**

In The March of Folly, *Barbara Tuchman, one of the century's finest historians, shows how easy it is to ignore the lessons of failure. This is especially true when the problems are self inflicted and we can find ways to justify our actions – at least to our own satisfaction. This tends not to be a problem for those who have faced difficulties and setbacks in their early career. They, like Lincoln, recognize that in order to get ahead they must first survive and then adapt to new circumstances.*

The March of Folly
by Barbara Tuchman

Mental standstill or stagnation – the maintenance intact by rulers and policy-makers of the ideas they started with – is fertile ground for folly. Montezuma is a fatal and tragic example. Leaders in government, on the authority of Henry Kissinger, do not learn beyond the convictions they bring with them; these are 'the intellectual capital they will consume as long as they are in office.' Learning from experience is a faculty almost never practised. Why did American experience of supporting the unpopular party in China supply no analogy to

Vietnam? And the experience of Vietnam none for Iran? And why has none of the above conveyed any inference to preserve the present government of the United States from imbecility in El Salvador? 'If men could learn from history, what lessons it might teach us!' lamented Samuel Coleridge. 'But passion and party blind our eyes, and the light which experience gives us is a lantern on the stern which shines only on the waves behind us.' The image is beautiful but the message misleading, for the light on the waves we have passed through should enable us to infer the nature of the waves ahead.

In its first stage, mental standstill fixes the principles and boundaries governing a political problem. In the second stage, when dissonances and failing function begin to appear, the initial principles rigidify. This is the period when, if wisdom were operative, re-examination and re-thinking and a change of course are possible, but they are rare as rubies in a backyard. Rigidifying leads to increase of investment and the need to protect egos; policy founded upon error multiplies, never retreats. The greater the investment and the more involved in it the sponsor's ego, the more unacceptable is disengagement. In the third stage, pursuit of failure enlarges the damages until it causes the fall of Troy, the defection from the Papacy, the loss of a trans-Atlantic empire, the classic humiliation in Vietnam.

Persistence in error is the problem. Practitioners of government continue down the wrong road as if in thrall to some Merlin with magic power to direct their steps. There are Merlins in early literature to explain human aberration, but freedom of choice does exist – unless we accept the Freudian unconscious as the new Merlin. Rulers will justify a bad or wrong decision on the ground, as a historian and partisan wrote of John F. Kennedy, that 'He had no choice,' but no matter how equal two alternatives may appear, there is always freedom of choice to change or desist from a counter-productive course if the policy-maker has the moral courage to exercise it. He is not a fated creature blown by the whims of Homeric gods. Yet to recognize error, to cut losses, to alter course, is the most repugnant option in government.

For a chief of state, admitting error is almost out of the question. The American misfortune during the Vietnam period was to have had Presidents who lacked the self-confidence for the grand withdrawal. We come back again to Burke: 'Magnanimity in politics is not seldom the truest wisdom, and a great Empire and little minds go ill together.' The test comes in recognizing when persistence in error has become self-damaging. A prince, says Machiavelli, ought always to be a great asker and a patient hearer of truth about those things of which he has inquired, and he should be angry if he finds that anyone has scruples about telling him the truth. What government needs is great askers.

★

Quotable Business
by Louis E. Boone

Few great leaders encountered defeats so consistently before enjoying ultimate victory as did this individual. A frequently reported listing of these failures includes the following:

- Failed in business in 1831
- Ran for the legislature and lost in 1832
- Failed once again in business in 1834
- Sweetheart died in 1835
- Had a nervous breakdown in 1836
- Lost a second political race in 1838
- Defeated for Congress in 1843
- Defeated for Congress in 1846
- Defeated for Congress in 1848
- Defeated for US Senate in 1855
- Defeated for Vice President in 1856
- Defeated for US Senate in 1858

The man was Abraham Lincoln, elected sixteenth president of the United States in 1860.

COPING WITH CRISES

Lincoln faced crises that would have crushed a lesser man. He tapped reservoirs of resilience and self-belief to go on. Sculley draws out the importance of setting an example to others when problems emerge. Clifford and Cavanagh make the point that winners know they are winners – even when they are losing. In the kind of crisis noted by Lee Iacocca, Fran's maxim is, 'When the going gets tough, the tough get going.'

©Copyright 1982 United Feature Syndicate, Inc.
Used by special permission.

Odyssey: From Pepsi to Apple
by John Sculley

When you're manoeuvring through a crisis, self-confidence is extremely important. At times, there may be no guarantees that you'll make it through. It's critical, then, to maintain your cool, not to panic, and to look for incremental wins that can be built upon and utilized to motivate further the organization.

Only concern yourself with those things that you can do something about. The things you can do something about shouldn't keep you awake at night. To keep a clear head, it's important to get some time off alone. You need perspective in a crisis. I gained it by getting up each morning at four-thirty for a long run on the road in the cold darkness.

After the key decisions were made, I felt quite calm – even in the most difficult and tense moments. The reason: I was starting to take control of those things that were controllable. I've often heard top athletes say that the actual event of competition is a calming experience that seems to unravel almost in slow motion. It's the few moments before the action that are the most difficult to deal with. I think this is true in a business crisis as well.

★

**If at first you don't succeed,
destroy all evidence that you tried.**

★

The Winning Performance
by D. K. Clifford Jr & R. E. Cavanagh

Responding to trouble

The best responses to adversity are reminiscent of the response of a golfer whose game is off: single-minded commitment, a tremendous sense of urgency, and a redoubling of time and attention to the basics. The underlying attitude of each is the same: I am a winner. I not only will solve this problem, but I'll be even stronger and better as a result.

The actions these companies take to recover from a stumble are as varied as the niches they compete in and the people who make up the companies. Sometimes they sell divisions that no longer show promise or meet financial standards. Sometimes they invest in new product lines or technology. Sometimes they reorganize to recapture their former simplicity by combining divisions with related products or markets – but if it makes sense, they also split up divisions to create smaller, more entrepreneurial, faster-response businesses. Some have doubled their research-and-development spending to regain a product advantage; others have put top priority on trimming the inefficiencies that crept into their cost structure during periods of high growth, severing unproductive people, but also adding new skills that may be key to coping with the new problems.

How the winners *don't* behave in times of trouble is as

illuminating as how they do. They steer clear of unsound business practices, such as shipping poor-quality products in order to generate short-term cash. They avoid unsound financial practices, such as overvaluing their inventories, booking sales to customers with poor credit, or using up important reserves. They don't indulge in shortsighted organizational steps, such as terminating people who will be needed in the future, or consolidating unlike businesses for ephemeral economies. They don't drop development programmes that are creating tomorrow's products and businesses; they don't assume, at least not without compelling evidence, that the problems will solve themselves if the company simply 'stays the course'. They follow common sense.

★

Iacocca: An Autobiography
by Lee Iacocca

... when you're in a crisis, there's no time to run a study. You've got to put down on a piece of paper the ten things that you absolutely have to do. That's what you concentrate on. Everything else – forget it. The spectre of dying has a way of focusing your attention in a big hurry.

At the same time, you've got to make sure you've got something left when the immediate crisis is over. That sounds simple enough, but it's much easier said than done. It takes gritting your teeth. It takes discipline. You hope and you pray that it works, because you're doing the best you can. You're concentrating on the future, meaning you hope you'll be alive tomorrow.

The willingness to act alone, especially in a crisis, does not blind successful managers to the value of advice. Mark McCormack points out that taking advice is a sign of strength, not weakness.

The 110% Solution
by Mark McCormack

Take my advice, please

You're never more vulnerable than at those moments when you need advice – when you realize you don't fully comprehend a situation and have to rely on someone else's judgment.

But you also are never more in control: you are the one who decides whom to turn to, how well to listen and how seriously to act on their counsel.

Some people aren't good at taking advice. They can't admit they need help. They can't accept that someone may know more than they do. They ask the wrong questions. They can't deal with conflicting advice. They only hear what they want to hear or what confirms their own opinion. They listen to the wrong people. Or to too many people. And even if they choose the right advisers, they misinterpret the advice, or don't believe it or only follow half of it.

Some people don't think taking advice is important. To them it is a sign of weakness rather than a necessary social skill. It is passive rather than active. No one congratulates you for being good at it. (When was the last time someone praised you for 'taking advice well?') In the advice game, we all would rather be perceived as the one dispensing wisdom rather than seeking it.

★

The Law of Probability Dispersal
Whatever hits the fan will not be evenly distributed.

'*Amazing! You should write a book.*'

Sources and Acknowledgements

The following is a list of books and articles from which excerpts have been included. These excerpts are reproduced by permission of the publisher shown, except where stated otherwise or where the original material is no longer in copyright.

If there are any omissions or misattributions of copyright, these are unintentional. Any such errors brought to the attention of Virgin Publishing will be corrected in a future edition.

Adair, John, *Effective Leadership*, Pan, London, 1983. Reprinted by permission of the Peters Fraser & Dunlop Group Ltd

Alletzhauser, Albert, *The House of Nomura*, published by Bloomsbury Publishing Ltd, 1989

Bernstein, David, *Company Image and Reality*, Holt Rinehart Winston. Reproduced by permission of Cassell Plc

Blanchard, Kenneth, and Johnson, Spencer, *The One Minute Manager*, Collins (an imprint of HarperCollins Publishers Ltd). Copyright © 1981, 1982 by Blanchard Family Partnership and Candle Communications Corp. By permission of William Morrow & Company, Inc.

Boone, Louis E., *Quotable Business*, Random House Inc.

Bowles, Colin, (ed.), *The Wit's Dictionary*. Reprinted by permission of Angus & Robertson Publishers

Branson, Richard, 'Risk Taking', *Journal of General Management*, Vol. II No. 2, Winter 1985

Burrough, Bryan, and Helyar, John, *Barbarians at the Gate*. Reprinted by permisson of Jonathan Cape, London, 1990 and HarperCollins Publishers Inc.

Byham, William C., and Cox, Jeff, *Zapp!*, Century Hutchinson, London, 1989

Cannon, Tom, *Basic Marketing*. Reproduced by permission of Cassell Plc, 1990

Cannon, Tom, *Enterprise*. Reproduced by permission of Butterworth-Heinemann Ltd

Clegg, Barbara, *The Man Who Made Littlewoods*, Hodder & Stoughton, 1993

Clifford, Donald K., Jr and Cavanagh, Richard E., *The Winning Performance*. Copyright © 1985 by Donald K. Clifford Jr and Richard E. Cavanagh. Used by permission of Bantam Books, a division of Bantam Doubleday Dell Publishing Group, Inc., and by permission of Sidgwick & Jackson

Clutterbuck, David, and Crainer, Stuart, *Makers of Management*, Macmillan London Ltd

Cox, D. F., 'Keeping Informed: Clues for Advertising Strategists', *Harvard Business Review*, Nov-Dec 1961. (Reprinted by permission of *Harvard Business Review*. Copyright © 1961 by the President and Fellows of Harvard College; all rights reserved.)

Crosby, Philip. B., *Quality Without Tears*, McGraw-Hill Inc., 1984

Dawkins, Richard, *The Selfish Gene*. Reprinted from the 2nd edition, 1989, by permission of Oxford University Press. © Richard Dawkins 1989

Drucker, Peter, *Managing for Results*. Reproduced by permission of Butterworth-Heinemann Ltd

Farwell, Byron, *Queen Victoria's Little Wars*. Reproduced by kind permission of the author

Forte, Charles, *Forte*, Sidgwick & Jackson, London, 1986

Goldsmith, Walter, and Clutterbuck, David, *The Winning Streak*. Copyright © Walter Goldsmith and David Clutterbuck 1985

Golzen, Godfrey, and Garner, Andrew, *Smart Moves*, Penguin Books, London, 1992, first published 1990. Copyright © Godfrey Golzen and Andrew Garner, 1990. Reproduced by permission of Penguin Books Ltd

Hammer, Michael, and Champy, James, *Reengineering the Corporation*. Copyright © 1993 by Michael Hammer and James Champy. Reprinted by permission of HarperCollins Publishers Inc.

Handy, Charles, *The Age of Unreason*, Business Books, London

Handy, Charles, *Understanding Organizations*, Penguin Books, Harmondsworth, 1976, third revised edition 1985. Copyright © Charles B. Handy, 1976, 1981, 1985. Reproduced by permission of Penguin Books Ltd

Hart, Christopher W. L., 'The Power of Unconditional Service Guarantees', *Harvard Business Review*, July-Aug 1988. (Reprinted by kind permission of *Harvard Business Review*. Copyright © 1988 by the President and Fellows of Harvard College; all rights reserved.)

Harvey-Jones, John, *Making It Happen*, Fontana (an imprint of HarperCollins Publishers Ltd)

Heller, Robert, *The Decision Makers*, Hodder & Stoughton and Penguin Books USA Inc.

Heller, Robert, *The Pocket Manager*, Hodder & Stoughton and Penguin Books USA Inc.

Horton, Thomas, and Reid, Peter, *Beyond the Trust Gap*, R. D. Irwin

Iacocca, Lee, with Novak, William, *Iacocca: An Autobiography*. Copyright © 1984 by Lee Iacocca. Used by permission of Bantam Books, a division of Bantam Doubleday Dell Publishing Group, Inc., and by permission of Sidgwick & Jackson

Ilich, John, *Deal Breakers and Breakthroughs*. Copyright © 1992 by John Ilich. Reprinted by permission of John Wiley & Sons, Inc.

Kanter, Rosabeth Moss, *The Changemasters*. Copyright © 1983 by Rosabeth Moss Kanter. Reprinted by permission of Simon & Schuster, Inc.

Kanter, Rosabeth Moss, *When Giants Learn to Dance*. Copyright © 1989 by Rosabeth Moss Kanter. Reprinted by permission of Simon & Schuster, Inc.

Kay, John, *Foundations for Corporate Success*. Reprinted by permission of Oxford University Press. © John Kay 1993

Kelly, Francis J., and Kelly, Heather M., *What They Really Teach You at the Harvard Business School*. Reprinted by permission of Warner Books, New York; and by permission of HarperCollins Publishers Ltd. Copyright © 1985 by Francis Kelly, Heather Mayfield Kelly and Jon Zonderman

Koren, Leonard, and Goodman, Peter, *The Haggler's Handbook: One Hour to Negotiating Power*. Reproduced by permission of Hutchinson and W. W. Norton & Company, Inc. Copyright © 1991 by Leonard Koren and Peter Goodman

Kotler, Philip, *Marketing Management*, Prentice-Hall, Englewood Cliffs, 1991

Kotler, Philip, 'From Sales Obsession to Marketing Effectiveness', *Harvard Business Review*, Nov-Dec 1977. (Reprinted by permission of *Harvard Business Review*. Copyright © 1977 by the President and Fellows of Harvard College; all rights reserved.)

Lacey, Robert, *Ford*, Heinemann, Oxford, 1987. Copyright Robert Lacey 1986. Reproduced by permission of Curtis Brown, London Ltd

Levitt, T., 'Exploiting the Product Life Cycle', *Harvard Business Review*, Nov-Dec 1967. (Reprinted by permission of *Harvard Business Review*. Copyright © 1967 by the President and Fellows of Harvard College; all rights reserved.)

McCormack, Mark, *The 110% Solution*. Reprinted by permission of Villard Books, a division of Random House Inc., and International Management Group

McCormack, Mark, *What They Don't Teach You at Harvard Business School*, Collins (an imprint of HarperCollins Publishers Ltd) and by permission of International Management Group

Mintzberg, Henry, *Mintzberg on Management*, Free Press, New York, 1989

Morpurgo, J. E., *Allen Lane: King Penguin*. Reproduced by permission of J. E. Morpurgo

Naipaul, V. S., *A House for Mr Biswas*, Penguin Books 1969, first published by Andre Deutsch 1961. Copyright © V. S. Naipaul, 1961, 1969. Reproduced by permission of Penguin Books Ltd

Naisbitt, John, and Aburdene, Patricia, *Re-inventing the Corporation*. Reprinted by permission of Warner Books, New York. Copyright © 1985 by John Naisbitt and Patricia Aburdene

Naumann, J., 'What Is Customer Driven Marketing?', reprinted from *Business Horizons*, Nov-Dec 1992. Copyright 1992 by the Foundation for the School of Business at Indiana University. Used with permission

Ohmae, Kenichi, *The Mind of the Strategist*, McGraw-Hill Inc., 1982

Parkinson, C. Northcote, *Parkinson's Law*, John Murray (Publishers) Ltd

Pascale, Richard, *Managing on the Edge*, Viking, London, 1990. Copyright © Richard Pascale, 1990. Reproduced by permission of Penguin Books Ltd

Peter, Laurence J. and Hull, Raymond, *The Peter Principle*. Copyright © 1969 by William Morrow & Company, Inc. By permission of William Morrow & Company, Inc.

Peter, Laurence J., *The Peter Pyramid*. Copyright © 1985 by Laurence J. Peter. By permission of William Morrow & Company, Inc. and HarperCollins Publishers Ltd

Peters, Tom, and Waterman, Robert, *In Search of Excellence*. (Copyright © 1982 by Thomas J. Peters and Robert H. Waterman Jr. Reprinted by permission of HarperCollins Publishers Inc.)

Peters, Tom, *Liberation Management*. Copyright © 1992 by Excel, a California Limited Partnership. Reprinted by permission of Alfred A. Knopf, Inc.

Peters, Tom, *Thriving on Chaos*. Copyright © 1987 by Excel, a California Limited Partnership. Reprinted by permission of Alfred A. Knopf, Inc.

Pirsig, Robert M., *Zen and the Art of Motorcycle Maintenance*, The Bodley Head, London and by permission of William Morrow & Company, Inc.

Porter, Michael, *Competitive Advantage*, Free Press, New York, 1985

Porter, Michael, *Competitive Strategy*, Free Press, New York, 1980

Potter, Stephen, *One-upmanship*. Reprinted by permission of the Peters, Fraser and Dunlop Group Ltd

Prahalad, C. K., and Hamel, G., 'The Core Competence of the Corporation', *Harvard Business Review*, May-June 1990. (Reprinted by permission of *Harvard Business Review*. Copyright © 1990 by the President and Fellows of Harvard College; all rights reserved.)

Reddin, William J., *Managerial Effectiveness*, McGraw-Hill Book Company Europe, 1970

Roddick, Anita, *Body and Soul*, Hutchinson, London, 1991

Schleh, Edward, *Management by Results*, McGraw-Hill Inc., 1961

Schumacher, E. F., *Small Is Beautiful*, Hutchinson, London

Scott, Bill, *Into Profit*, McGraw-Hill Book Company Europe

Sculley, John, *Odyssey: From Pepsi to Apple*. Copyright © 1987 by John Sculley. Reprinted by permission of HarperCollins Publishers Inc.

Sloan, Alfred P., *My Years with General Motors*. Reproduced by permission of Sidgwick & Jackson

Sloma, Richard S., *Getting It to the Bottom Line*, reprinted with the permission of The Free Press, a Division of Macmillan, Inc. Copyright © 1987 by The Free Press

Smiles, Samuel, *Self-Help*, 1856

Stalk, George, and Hout, Thomas M., *Competing Against Time*, reprinted with the permission of The Free Press, a division of Macmillan, Inc. Copyright © 1990 by The Free Press

Sugar, Alan, *Alan Sugar: The Amstrad Story*, Hutchinson, London, 1990

Toffler, Alvin, *Across the Board*, Bantam, New York, 1991

Townsend, Robert, *Further Up the Organisation*, Michael Joseph, London, 1984. Copyright © 1970, 1984 by Robert Townsend. Reprinted by permission of Alfred A. Knopf, Inc. and Michael Joseph Ltd

Tuchman, Barbara, *The March of Folly*, Penguin, London, 1984

Voss, Christopher A., *Just in Time Manufacture*, IFS International Ltd

Wallace, James, and Erickson, Jim, *Hard Drive: Bill Gates and the Making of the Microsoft Empire*. Copyright © 1992 by James Wallace and Jim Erickson. Reprinted by permission of John Wiley & Sons, Inc.

Walton, Mary, *Deming Management at Work*. Reprinted by permission of Mercury Books and The Putnam Publishing Group. Copyright © 1990 by Mary Walton

Wolfe, Tom, *The Bonfire of the Vanities*, Jonathan Cape, London

Womack, J. P., Jones, P. T., and Roos, D., *The Machine That Changed the World*, reprinted with the permission of Rawson Associates, an imprint of Macmillan Publishing Co. Copyright © 1990 James P. Womack, Daniel T. Jones, Daniel Roos and Donna Sammons Carpenter

Yergin, Daniel, *The Prize*. Copyright © 1991, 1992 by Daniel Yergin. Reprinted by permission of Simon & Schuster, Inc.

Young, Arthur, *The Manager's Handbook*, first published in 1986, copyright © Marshall Editions Ltd 1986

Zeithaml, V., Parasuraman, A., and Berry, L., *Delivering Quality Service*, reprinted with the permission of The Free Press, a Division of Macmillan, Inc. Copyright © 1990 by The Free Press

Zuboff, Shoshana, *In the Age of the Smart Machine*. Reproduced by permission of Butterworth-Heinemann Ltd

I am grateful to the following for permission to reproduce cartoons:

Ashleigh Brilliant (cartoons on pages 46, 119 and 146: POT-SHOTS copyright Ashleigh Brilliant, Santa Barbara, California, reproduced by permission of the author)

Business Humour Ltd (cartoons on pages 36, 171, 178, 182 and 197)

King Features (cartoon appearing on page 209: reprinted with special permission of King Features Syndicate)

Nicholas Brealey Publishing Ltd, London (for cartoon on page 150: this previously appeared in *Build a Better Life by Stealing Office Supplies: Dogbert's Big Book of Business* by Scott Adams)

Punch magazine (cartoons appearing on pages 25, 81, 85, 105, 110, 130, 134, 136, 143, 190, 204, 218, 220 and 252)

The Saturday Evening Post (cartoons appearing on pages 34, 70, 166, 225 and 231)

United Media (cartoons appearing on pages 150, 223, 235 and 248)

Index of Authors

Airline of the Year 1991

Airline of the Year 1992

Airline of the Year 1993

APPARENTLY THE JUDGES WERE INFLUENCED BY CHAMPAGNE, LIMOS AND STIMULATING MASSAGES.

Bribery? Corruption? Dirty tricks? No way. We're just describing our normal Upper Class service. Although with the door-to-door limos, in-flight masseuse, Raymond Blanc cuisine, huge, comfy seats, non-stop champagne and free flights, it's anything but normal. What's more, it costs no more than an ordinary Business Class ticket. Which is probably why readers of Executive Travel have voted us 'Airline of the Year' for 3 years on the trot. But don't just take their word for it – call us on 0293 747 500 and judge for yourself.

Upper Class  *Virgin* atlantic